# Forgive Us This Day Our Daily Bread

*Can A Comfortable Church Remember Jesus?*

# Forgive Us This Day Our Daily Bread

*Can A Comfortable Church Remember Jesus?*

Chad Hale

iv

This book is dedicated to Ella Duffy Haynes, one of the coordinators of the food cooperatives for low-income families formed by Georgia Avenue Church, who died August 7, 2019, and to four other coordinators, Jackie Palmer, Fay Romero, Kenny Redding and Spanga Gwabeni, and to Brian. And finally, to my wife, Barbara Antonoplos.

Front cover: photo by Barbara Antonoplos; wooden cross carved by John Pickens; back cover: author photo by Johnathon Kelso

# Table of Contents

1 God presides in the heavenly council; in the assembly of the gods he gives his decision.

2 "You must stop judging unjustly; you must no longer be partial to the wicked!

3 Defend the rights of the poor and the orphans; be fair to the needy and the helpless.

4 Rescue them from the power of evil people. ...

8 Come, O God, and rule the world; all the nations are yours.

Psalm 82 (TEV)

[Jesus] stood up to read,[17]and the scroll of the prophet Isaiah was given to him. He unrolled the scroll and found the place where it was written: [18]"The Spirit of the Lord is upon me, because he has anointed me to bring good news to the poor. He has sent me to proclaim release to the captives and recovery of sight to the blind, to let the oppressed go free, [19]to proclaim the year of the Lord's favor." [20]And he rolled up the scroll, gave it back to the attendant, and sat down. The eyes of all in the synagogue were fixed on him. [21]Then he began to say to them, "Today this scripture has been fulfilled in your hearing."

Luke 4:16-21 (NRSV)

# Preface

This book is predominantly a book of stories, stories from an urban pastor, primarily in the form of newsletters sent out over a period of about twenty years. The stories relate to Georgia Avenue Church in Atlanta, Georgia, and the food co-ops for low-income families that were formed out of the church. These particular stories cover a period of time from about 1981 to middle 2002, before our community outreach work (Georgia Avenue Community Ministry) became separate from Georgia Avenue Church as its own nonprofit (now known as "Urban Recipe").

There are so many to whom I am grateful, particularly in relation to the stories that prompt this publication. First of all, my wife, Barbara, and then our two children, Helen and John. Barbara was a good and faithful editor of many of my letters, managing to spare my dear readers much tortuous prose, though, as you will see, I still managed to slip some in. Since for a number of years these letters were sent out strictly via the postal service, my youngest children were often my helpers to accomplish that task. Thank you, dear family.

I am grateful to the Lord for calling me to this place and work. I am grateful to the people here, named and unnamed in these stories, who have taught me so much. This place is a neighborhood that, unbelievably to me, some are still wary of because of its one-time reputation for crime, even though there is no longer a need for fear, given the changes that have taken place. When I began, despite the problems and material poverty, it actually was a place of great richness, richness that most middle-class folks did not know about or even want to know about. I have learned much; I have gained much.

Given that people had offered to support our work by praying and/or sending funds, volunteering, etc., I had to communicate with them, which I did through a (mostly) monthly mailing. Typically, in the early years, that would be a one-page vignette relating recent experiences. Over time, some of those who supported these efforts encouraged me to circulate the letters farther afield. I have not taken that task to heart until now, but I do so here, trusting my dear friends' prompting. So, I thank you who have been persistent about pushing me to share these stories more widely.

I am also grateful to the many people who have made it possible for me to live and work here. I have endeavored to be faithful with regard to their kindness and generosity. I am very appreciative of those who supported our work in small or large ways, in many cases, generously and faithfully for long periods.

Chad Hale, August 2019
Atlanta, Georgia

# Introduction

My experience as a middle-class white male in the United States is that it is difficult to love my neighbor as myself. My experience is also that it is life-giving to make the effort. Perhaps I more naturally do better at it if I define "neighbor" very narrowly, confining it to "folks like me," but Jesus has not allowed me to do that.

So that is what this book is about—my sense of "call" as a Christian pastor to love my neighbor as myself, and my answer to that call. It is about my journey across the chasm between being a moderately "have" person, middle-class, male, white and well educated, though never financially wealthy as such, to the other side where poverty is concentrated and there is abundant need. Oddly, in doing so I have become a rich man. So maybe this is actually a book about prosperity theology that should be titled, *How to Get "Rich" Off of Poor People.* Ah, but of what kind of wealth do I speak? That you will learn as you read.

Beyond my personal sense of call, my larger concern is that the mainstream church in the USA tends to organize itself so as to avoid loving those neighbors who are "the least." I fear that it has, to a great extent, joined the larger society in its willingness to abandon those who are poor, and is doing so not just at the peril of the poor, but at its own peril. The church in large measure minimizes Jesus' concern for the poor or turns his concern into rather cheap and easy charity as a way to avoid the call of Jesus to love one another as he has loved us. Jesus' plan, as I understand the picture in the New Testament, is that rich and poor will be together (and, after all, so many of those who are in need are Christian brothers and sisters), learning from and caring for each other, not separated and isolated as classes and races as we tend to be now. This is Jesus' way to make sure those who are in need have the necessities of life and joyful community, and those who are comfortable don't become ensnared by their treasures and lose their lives. There is no doubt it is a struggle to be together with disparities and differences, but I believe that the struggle is important and one of the primary tools the Lord uses to sanctify and transform us.

For my part, I have been blessed to have many teachers along the way. I think you will find their stories to be of interest. I will begin with a snapshot of the church and a story about one of my most important teachers and her family.

# Section 1

# Two-Family Constance

I have lived and worked in southeast Atlanta most of the time since 1978. When I first came here, the area was one that many white people had fled. The area, once largely middle-middle class city workers, is close to downtown, within walking distance of the capitol building. When we moved here it was mostly poorer people—long-time homeowners, and renters in apartments and rooming houses owned by absentee landlords.

I am a Protestant American Baptist pastor. Born in Dallas, Texas, I began life as a Southern Baptist, but over time realized there were things about the way that denomination practiced its discipleship with which I did not agree. It began to be clear to me that to too much of the church I was around, "love your neighbor as yourself" mostly meant "love your white neighbor as yourself" and treat others the same way the surrounding culture does—abysmally. For me, that was a problem.

In 1981, I helped form a new church, Georgia Avenue Church, in the Grant Park neighborhood of Atlanta, and was asked to be a pastor to that body. The long-time Presbyterian congregation in the building had disbanded, but there was a ministry that had continued to make use of the space. The most public and consistent activity of that program was a lunch served every Wednesday to anyone who needed a meal. The program was founded and directed by Louise Probst, wife of the Rev. Fred Probst who had been the pastor at the nearby Capitol Avenue Baptist Church, a Southern Baptist church. I was told that when he passed, the program had to move because the church would no longer allow Louise to serve African-American children in the building. ("Love your white neighbor as yourself!") So, she searched until she found a home at the Georgia Avenue Presbyterian Church, which offered space in the "fellowship hall," with kitchen attached. Over time, as Louise aged, the church inherited her ministry, and as the neighborhood population shifted, the attendees also shifted from largely poor families with many children to primarily homeless men.

Georgia Avenue Church, which still meets, has never been over a hundred people, always has had a quite diverse membership, and was originally situated in the midst of much poverty and need. For the church and me to engage in the larger community work other funding and support was needed beyond what the church itself could provide. Other people began to make financial contributions to support our community work—work that over time predominantly became the formation of food cooperatives for low-income families. The food co-ops are still in operation, providing food security and supportive community to people in need.

I don't remember the church without Constance; she was present almost from the start. We were her second family. She had mental challenges from birth. She was the second of twins, though no twin was expected. The story goes that after the first babe, Connie, was born, sometime later the attending physicians figured out there was a second child, who came into the world with the umbilical cord wrapped around her neck. The medical authorities claimed she would never walk. She began to walk when she was 5 and she never stopped.

Constance had a patent on mosey. And she was overweight—a lot. As an adult she weighed 350-400 pounds, so she lumbered and shuffled around the neighborhood. She was amazing in a way; she had to be super strong, because she would carry that weight around all over the place, walking for long periods of time throughout the neighborhood and beyond. Her twin, Connie, was attractive and trim. One would never guess they were twins.

She loved her large family and her church. She was manipulative and needy, but she had such a good heart. One of the most painful things for Constance was that she was not only mentally "slow," as she used to say; she *knew* she was mentally "slow," and she hated it.

Constance's father, Big Hawk, was the kingpin drug dealer of the area, the one freighting the goods in. He owned four lots with two houses along a stretch three blocks from me. In a previous era, he would throw pig roasts for the neighborhood. He had a bunch of vehicles, one of which was a long black Cadillac limousine with a TV. Early on, he didn't want Constance going to church, so he would whip her to stop her from attending. It didn't work.

In 1984 Constance asked me to go with her to visit her father who was in jail. Constance was 22 at the time. I had never met Big Hawk but I was willing to go with her. I knew hardly anything about him, but I had heard of him for sure; one of the men who came to our Wednesday lunch worship service and meal was crippled and walked with a cane from being in a gunfight with Hawk. Big Hawk and I stood across from each other, separated by glass and steel, and talked through phone receivers.

Well, something happened in that meeting. The Lord moved in Big Hawk's spirit, and he became a Christian—unbeknownst to me!

Constance reported that Hawk wanted to see me again. When I went to the jail, he told me that when I had visited the first time, he thought I was some kind of undercover policeman, but when he was holding the receiver it was as though the receiver were electrified and it was burning his hand, and when we prayed he felt something happening to him. At the time I didn't know any of this. I learned it at that next visit when Hawk said he was giving up the drugs, he would be at church when he got out, and he was going to follow the Lord.

Jailhouse religion is its own genre. You never know where it's headed. A lot of people get it; for some it's real. In jail, people are in a situation in which they have to stop; they are desperate and they may assess their lives, but above all, they want out of jail. For Hawk, it was real—not easy, not a straight path, but real. He never went back to the drugs. In ways, he was hard to live with, hard to be around, but he was for real.

His conversion was difficult for everybody who

came in touch with him, but especially his family. Big Hawk had been rich; his family, including his twenty-three kids by I don't remember how many women, all had what they needed. I met some of the women and a number of the children. He claims that when he was arrested the police toted hundreds of thousands of dollars in cash out of his house. As I said, once he came to the Lord, he did not go back to the life that had brought him those riches, so he was no longer rich—in fact, he was dirt poor. In order to keep going, he stooped so low as to shine shoes in downtown Atlanta. Mostly he tried to find cement or masonry work, which was his skill, but he struggled big time, and just as he pushed his family members to turn to the Lord, except for Constance they pushed back for him to return to the drugs. They all wanted the "good life" that the drugs had afforded and they wanted back the old Big Hawk.

He didn't turn back and they didn't convert. Meanwhile, like so many converts, Hawk became judgmental and pushy with his newfound faith, wanting his family to experience the new reality that had grasped him, but pushing them away all the more in his efforts to convert them. He eventually got over that, but he did some damage. His wife became totally disaffected and ultimately died from her addictions. She was already into drugs, for which Hawk blamed himself; she would go into rages and take a bat to what he had left of his vehicles. She became one angry woman.

Going from being big shots to nobodies was hard on the whole family. Most of the kids (all grown by that time, but still an intimate part of a clan) never got over it. They grew up benefiting from drugs; now the drugs or finding ways to survive took them down. James died of AIDS; Harriet served ten years in jail for "cruelty to children" (a charge she vehemently denies); Connie got into drugs and prostitution and died of AIDS in her mid-thirties; Marlene was on drugs (which she eventually got free of) and had 8 children. Jerome, who had a good job in another state and was a football player, who says he was given a tryout by a pro team, got back into drugs, left his family, and died early of cancer; LaKing was addicted and died in his 50's from ulcers; Monica ("Fat") had ten children, got free of the drugs and earned her way in the world by running a cleaning business. All the girls had their children taken by the Georgia Department of Family and Children Services, either temporarily or permanently. The Hawkins children struggled, to say the least. But Constance, the one born damaged, the one who went to church, the one who was so loving, who was the reason her Dad came to the Lord, did not become addicted. She became an artist under the tutelage of Donna Pickens, an artist in our church, and her paintings were displayed in galleries in Atlanta and New York. She got her own place in a public high rise, actually had a part-time job and managed to pray for and minister to others. In some strange way she was "saved" by her congenital damage. She wasn't in demand for her body; she never had any interest in drugs. She was just a very slow, manipulative, good-hearted member of our church and community.

Constance died of a heart attack in her apartment, alone, in the early morning hours of Thanksgiving, 2003. I hate that she was alone; she was alone so much, and she hated that, too, since she had grown up in such a large family. She loved having people around, and would come to me periodically talking about how she was going to get pregnant because she wanted a baby! But Constance had to live alone in her own space as part of the rules of the public high rise. And truthfully, since she was on disability and got money every month, and since her brothers and sisters were so often needy, some of them pressured her to let them stay with her and give them money, and some of them would be mean about it, so she needed to be in a controlled living environment where they could not take as much advantage of her. She was 41 when she died. Death at an early age is a feature of our community.

I conducted the funeral service. The sanctuary was packed; so many people knew and loved Constance. It was amazing to see all those people, some I didn't know or had no idea had known Constance, and to hear them speak during the open mic time of how she had affected them. One after another spoke, including a City Councilwoman, lawyers, you name it, all present to grieve this overweight nobody who moseyed around southeast Atlanta.

Constance endured much: at times our impatience with her neediness; being alone; her mental struggles; being poor; being African-American. (One Sunday morning during the worship "sharing time," Constance took the floor to inform us, "Racism pisses me off!") Most of us thought we were better than Constance, but when it came to the heart, she was ahead of us all. It was an honor to know her; the Lord was reaching out to me and to all of us through this sweet, needy woman. Sometimes I can still see her great mass moving down the street and I can see her huge face light up with her fantastic smile, and I can hear her pray her simple, heartfelt, compassionate prayers. I miss her.

So when I was getting ready for her funeral service, I was grieving. I didn't know what to say. I took my son to baseball practice and went to a Burger King down the hill to wait for him and try to write. As I prayed and thought about Constance, a moment came when I began to write, and I knew it was from the Lord, for which I am so thankful. Something about these words is true and real. Here is the eulogy, complete with scriptural references, which I delivered at Constance's service on December 5, 2003.

(The Scriptures were drawn from the Advent season—Isaiah11:1-9; Isaiah 53:1-3; and Hebrews13:1-3)

So the Lord God called all the heavenly host together, and said, "I need a volunteer for a special assignment, a very difficult assignment." Many angelic beings stepped forward.

One asked, "Where in the universe, O Lord, will this assignment be?"

"On the planet Earth in the Milky Way galaxy." More than half of the angels stepped back: "We don't want to go to that dark planet," they said. "It is full of strife and discord."

The ones who were left asked, "What would we do there, Lord?"

"You will go to an area of conflict, where the evil one has set people against people, based on color and class, wealth and education, any reason they can find to be divided and isolated and self-centered. You will go to break through that self-centeredness, to overcome divisions, to teach people to love, so whoever goes must have much love for these crippled beings."

More of the angelic beings stepped back; now there were only three left.

"OK, Lord, we can do that," they said.

"There is no 'we'—whoever goes will go alone," said the Lord.

So the remaining three shuffled nervously and asked more questions. One especially was persistent: "So we will need to be armed and ready. With what will you equip one of us? I'm sure I would be a man, strong and powerful for this war, to take blows I will receive and then for people to admire."

"No, you will not be a man—you will be what they foolishly call the 'weaker sex;' you will be a woman."

"Ah, well, then you will make her extremely beautiful, so that the people will be moved by her comeliness to love when they see her."

"No, whoever goes will not be beautiful according to their standards. The majority of those people there have set up false standards, and they think slim and light skinned is beautiful. You will not be slim and light; you will be dark skinned and heavy set."

"Well, then you can still give that heavy body shapeliness and good health so that I will have something I can hold up to attract an audience."

"No, you will be ugly to their eyes, overweight and unshapely and your health will be very bad. Your body will be a burden to you, too, a kind of prison. You will have to endure much."

"But, even so, couldn't I be fast and athletic, so that people will see how agile I am and I can give glory to God for my abilities and witness to people how you love?"

"No, you will be slow, not able to run at all and even slow when you walk. You will meander sluggishly all over the neighborhood as a sign to people that I am with them. And you will be awkward."

"Wow, this *is* hard. Okay, so what strengths will you give someone then? Would you make me real smart, full of education, with a keen mind, so that I can convince people, that despite my looks and ill health, that you are love?"

"No, you will not be smart, you will hardly be able to read, and your mind will be damaged so that you will not be able to convince anyone by fine arguments about love. People will make fun of you, you will be the butt of their jokes and their irritation, and in that way, some will eventually see their lack of love, the evil in their hearts, and repent. You will be the recipient of their arrogance and judgmentalism and impatience. And not only that, you will know that you are damaged mentally and it will be a source of pain and grief for you."

"Well, then, you must be going to give whoever volunteers *something*, perhaps wealth, so at least some people will be attracted to me because of my money and I can teach them your ways."

"No, you will have no money, you will be poor and you will have little or nothing to offer anyone materially."

"Well, if we wouldn't have any attributes of our own, would you give us many children to share care with, a household full of love and joy?"

"Not that either. In your adult life you will be alone, and your main source of comfort will be something they call 'food,' and even that will betray you and add to your misery. But you will also have joy and laughter and love."

So, they said, "Well, Lord, that doesn't sound like enough—this seems too difficult. What would we have then to accomplish this task?"

"Nothing but poverty on every front; you will be childlike and you will have only your vulnerability and my spirit. But slowly others will come to see that you are an angel, that you are full of love, and they will learn from you and come to love you and care for you. You will not possess any of those attributes or possessions people prize and fight over, but your faithfulness and suffering will be what teaches others as you persist and are tenacious in your love for people and for me. I cannot lie to you; this assignment will not be fun, because people's first inclination will not be to love you, but to pity you yet keep their distance. Will any of you accept it?"

Two of the three stepped back, and said, "No, Lord, we could not do it. It is too much." Only one was left, and that angel hesitated, but said, "Yes, I will accept the assignment."

"Good. Great will be your reward in heaven. Now, I will give you this name as a sign: you will be called "Constance," and tenacious you will be, day in and day out, faithful to your task, unswerving. You will constantly be present, always calling on the phone, always in the way, always in need, reminding people of your loneliness and poverty, but you will nearly always be loving and gentle. And you will be a prophet, and your mantra, your word will be, "I just want to be uhsepted (sic) for who I is and who I'm are."

"But, Lord, that's not even good English."

"I know, but people will remember it better that way. You will love despite being abused and brushed off, and you will get hurt easily, and you will be lonely. You will be a pointer to me, and a reminder that will break people free of their false judgments, their fast-paced ways, and they will see you and slow down to listen to you and they will remember things other than their need to do business as usual. You will break through many hard hearts and overcome divisions, you will bring black people and white people together, I will use you to turn your earthly father from his evil, and when I bring you home, you will die of a broken heart (which they will call a "massive coronary attack"), and many people on earth will gather to honor you, and thank God for you, that you have visited them, and that you endured and taught them so much about my ways.

And so, the angel took the assignment, which she has just completed, and she was taken home, and here we are, gathered to remember Constance our Teacher and give thanks and praise to God for such a gift, grateful that she has touched our lives. Thank you, Constance, for enduring, and forgive us our slowness to learn.

Yes, we know Constance had her faults and wasn't perfect, but truthfully, in another way, she *was* perfect—she was just the way Constance was supposed to be. She was a perfect Constance and she endured great pain gracefully. This area of Atlanta has lost a powerful presence.

Let us pray together:

We thank you, O God, for our sister Constance, who in her way was so much like our brother Jesus. Forgive us our hardness of heart, and aid us, O Lord, to keep learning from her. You have touched us through her, for which we are very grateful. We are comforted in the knowledge that now she can rest, and her holidays will be continuous and be filled with the people she cared for so much. We grieve for ourselves, for our loss; console us, and grant to us a determination to live your ways of love with perseverance. Come Holy Spirit, and come quickly, Lord Jesus. Amen.

We thought we were her teachers, but all the while she was teaching us. It turns out we were the slow learners.

# Section 2

# Monthly Letters

Since our food cooperatives hold such a prominent place in the following letters, some explanation is necessary, which I offer here by contrasting our food co-op model to a typical food pantry in our area. Painting with a broad brush, at food pantries, individuals approach and are handed a bag of food that lasts a couple of days. Often having waited a long time in line, they receive food put together by church or other volunteers and then leave, having been treated well, or maybe not, and they cannot return for a month. The recipients usually have no choice about what they receive, and make no contribution to the effort, which reportedly can feel demeaning. While this type of set-up can provide much needed food in a crisis, it does not address the long-term need for food that burdens so many in our society. At their best, food pantries provide a temporary blessing; at their worst they allow a way for the givers to "do good" without having to actually engage the recipients as neighbors, enabling the givers to feel righteous while keeping a safe distance.

In our food cooperatives, we do not deal solely with individuals. The people in need become part of a cooperative community (50 member-families in each), taking on the responsibility to run their co-op and make sure it succeeds. These are people whose yearly household incomes, on average, are less than $12,000, and for a program fee of $4.00 per meeting they receive between $3,500 and $6,000 worth of food in a year. Meeting every other week year-round, in addition to receiving enough food to help provide true food security, members build long-term relationships and gain support that they didn't have before; they experience dignity, stability, empowerment, and joy—qualities of life that everyone, whether rich or poor, hungers for.

These letters focus on the overall co-op program and the co-op members to whom I have been blessed to relate over these years, and also draw on the life of Georgia Avenue Church and the Wednesday lunch program. In most cases, but not all, names have been changed, and where they have not, it is with the permission, sometimes urging, of the persons named. Some of these letters have been rendered to you in full, thinking they will convey an idea of the overall flow of our lives. From others I have extracted excerpts, judging that parts of the letter did not make sense to include. I have made edits on rare occasions to make matters clearer or perhaps to update certain information, but primarily have let the letters stand as originally written. There are gaps in the dates for various reasons. There were times I did not manage to actually write a letter every month but also, some letters were so concerned with administrative matters I did not consider them to be of value for purposes of this volume. Finally, I have lost at least one and perhaps others from what was my pre-computer era. These letters cover the period from the beginning of our food cooperatives up to the point when the Georgia Avenue Community Ministry transitioned from being an outreach of Georgia Avenue Church to being a separate nonprofit organization (which, as of 2014, adopted the name Urban Recipe). I have decided for the most part to roll them out without further comment, apart from a few updates included in footnotes.

The first letter, not placed chronologically but according to my awareness of the tensions between those who are comfortable and those who are not, gives an indication of some of the dynamics present in a ministry that was stretched between people who were in need and people who were not, truthfully between different worlds and worldviews, between which it was as if there was a tangible chasm. The particular incident the letter reports is about a meeting we had with representatives of a foundation to which we had applied for funding. It is noteworthy that in an odd way we did not get off on a good footing even before we met. The person who called us to set up the appointment was a nice enough young woman but we had a difficult time settling on a meeting date. She finally told me that she was trying to set the meeting on a day that looked as though it would be rainy because the Board member from their foundation, a retired corporate executive who was going to meet with us, lived on a lake and did not like to be away from the lake on sunny days! We did finally settle on a date that was predicted to be rainy, and as you will note, he came with his presuppositions about what we should be doing and how poor people should be, I will say, managed. One degree or another of that tension pervades our work, both with regard to people from outside our ministry and from within our own selves.

So, to repeat, the different themes of these letters are primarily: the community and work that were centered on the formation of our food co-ops; stories and events related to our people's lives; my own development in various ways; the richness and struggles of those who are economically poor and culturally distinctive, and the contrasts of their situations with the more middle and upper-class cultural norms and expectations which surround them. In our situation there are the peculiarities related to class, but also the strong racial prejudices and biases of southern society, which, of course, with varying degrees and patterns infect our total society.

April 28, 1993

Dear Friends and Relatives:

Please note the enclosed flyer about a fundraising concert that will take place May 16. If you can come, please do, and of course, feel free to invite others.

This past week my assistant and I met with three people from a foundation to which we had applied for $10,000. It did not turn out too well. The main concern voiced by the man, who seemed in charge, was, "how are we doing at getting these poor people down here to change?" It became clear that to him, "change" meant, "having fewer children," "getting off the dole," "getting jobs," etc. It also became clear he was not too interested in giving to efforts that aren't, as he sees it, manifesting the kind of changes he feels are called for.

I am not perfect, and we can learn from other people; however, the attitude of this man angered me. A retired executive, he came to this meeting from his lakeside home and a life totally removed from the realities of the lives of people here, and within minutes was telling us what we need to be doing to change "these people;" how we need to "scheme" to get them doing what's "best for them" ... and he claims to know what that is.

In ways this encounter was good for me: I sometimes forget how frighteningly narrow can be the thinking of those who are removed, especially those who are afflicted with power and wealth. They think they have "answers" for other people's lives. It was sobering. But in truth, I came to this work thinking more similarly to this man than I would like to admit—it is a common middle-class way to play God. Now I am clear that we cannot be doing the work of God beginning from such a standpoint. In twelve years of serving in this community, I have seen frustration, but no fruit, borne of this approach. Basically, it is an attitude of disdain, not care. Besides, fundamentally we are not here to *change* people—the Lord didn't teach us to change our neighbor, but to *love* our neighbor. And in so doing, we rub against and change each other, and openness comes to the One who does bring newness and life-giving change.

"Today's" golden rule is "those who have the gold make the rules." Since we don't want their rules...! Oh, well.... We really could have used that money, too.

The garden is just getting "off the ground." (As I wrote that phrase, something about it struck me funny—a garden off the ground!) The extension service people have been great. Marco, from Honduras, is the person assigned to work with us, and he knows gardens and gets along well with all of us. He had the dirt tested and said it was the best they had tested. (It's black dirt, not red clay!) The land's been plowed, we've cleaned it up, and Marco has marked out several plots 4 by 25, putting down wood chips in between. It looks good. The garden is another way for us to interact and grow together—plus have more food. There will be six gardeners—our projects tend to start small and grow.

The garden is one more means of living together, building alternative community. And, yes, change does take place, in all of us, but it is by God's grace, not our scheming.

November 1991

Dear Friends and Relatives:

Much of the Black population and some of the White around the church building are decimated by poverty coupled with drugs, high unemployment, alcoholism, single-parent families, children being neglected, even abused, prostitution. These people come to the Wednesday noon meal held each week at the church and nearly all say they "believe in Jesus." Many speak of Georgia Avenue as "my church"—they come to the meals, sometimes to the Wednesday worship service, at times seeking assistance and occasionally pastoral care from the church. A few of them are members of the Sunday congregation as well.

I have been uncomfortable that so much of the interaction with these members of the community revolves around charity, since it has no dignity in it for them and locks us into relating in unhealthy ways. Out of my desire to move beyond charity and take marginalized people seriously as brothers and sisters, I have prayed and searched for some structure that would move us to a place of *equality*, of working *together* to meet the needs.

But the greatest need, the need which most concerns me, is people's lack of belief in themselves and the lack of power in their professed belief that our Lord loves them and will listen if they cry out.

After consulting with people at the Wednesday lunch meetings and others, the means chosen to address the need was to form an organization in which we can work together as equals, in the name of Jesus Christ, to meet a genuine, specific and immediate need. The organization we formed is a *food cooperative* with voluntary membership.

Overarching *goal*: That calling on God in a conscious

way our people become empowered with the sense of God's love and their own and each other's worth, beauty and giftedness through working together in the name of Christ to obtain the things they need. Secondarily, the organization will function to some degree as an alternate community within the broken one in which they find themselves.

The *strategy* to reach these goals, again, is to form a food cooperative which will immediately put food in people's pantries, but which is also an organization that they will progressively come to control. An additional facet of the organization is that it is counted as a partner in the Georgia Avenue Church building and given space and expected to carry its own weight to keep the building maintained and functioning, so the cooperative already has some responsibilities and respect.

Secondly, as people become more responsible and the organization stronger, the cooperative will be the springboard for the members to brainstorm other programs and structures and the means through which they can work to carry out those plans and dreams.


January 1992

Dear Friends and Relatives:

The Georgia Avenue Food Co-operative continues to grow, but this presents problems. We have brought in more household members since I first wrote you, now having 55. However, the waiting list is already back up to about 70 households! We must stop adding names to a waiting list.

The people who are members of the co-op are "no 'count" in this society—the folks many get angry at for supposedly making government costs high because of food stamps and welfare. People say, "They ought to be working," but, of course, right now in our society there are not enough jobs for even middle-class people! But the co-op members are great—they come to the meetings, generally on time, do their part and more to make the co-op work. We have orderly meetings as a rule with growing respect for one another and what we are doing. The elected Steering

Committee meets faithfully to pray and debate directions. I must say, it is a joy to me to be part of it.

But we are too successful, and the need is too great. We cannot get larger in this present co-op. Any more people and we cannot maintain order in meetings; any more people and we cannot get the food here that we need with the trucks we have available. Yet here are the people, waiting, in need of food. But were we to add people, we would have to form a *second co-op*. That is all well and fine, *but* it is a *lot more work*. Paper work, in particular, which falls primarily on my assistant, is enormous. We do not as of now have the money for food, plus, and primarily, expanding our numbers clashes with the co-op becoming a *self-development* organization. Self-development requires a stable, set group that can brainstorm and plan and work together; expansion puts the energy into getting the food here and doing all the organizational work to keep going. So, we cannot further expand at the moment. We cannot sacrifice the goal of self-development, but it tugs at my heart to have to close the door to expansion. It is a shame we have such need.

I thank you for your responses of interest, concern and giving. This letter effort does not begin to raise the other half of support I need, but it helps enormously and I am so grateful to you. I must spend a good deal of time doing the funding work, which is a distraction, but right now a necessary one. I must keep approaching funding sources with proposals—at present it is definitely day-to-day, but I am confident the Lord will make a way for us.

With each letter I will send an envelope for your ease if you have made a financial commitment to my work. If you have said you would send a one-time gift or cannot make a financial pledge but wanted to receive my letter, I include an envelope, but it is not to put pressure on you—I just can't keep matters straight! So please be patient with me about this, as I am new at it.

May the Lord bless you in the New Year.

February 1992

Dear Friends and Relatives:

The Georgia Avenue Food Co-operative is the linchpin of my work in the community, the part that is most exciting.

We are clearly at a 2nd stage—we have grown all we can and still maintain order in our meetings and transport the food. We had reached a juncture—I felt it important to make sure that the co-op members *really* do want to move toward *self-development*—i.e. are they interested in exploring what else they can do. We voted on it—the members voted overwhelmingly to move in those directions.

*But*, at that same meeting, when we were handing out the food at the end, we had a great deal of chaos, and some people's food was stolen! Some of this stealing was done by others who came in to see what was going on—but some of it was done by members of the co-op! A great meeting ended up being a bit of a downer.

But that is part of our life. The Steering Committee decided we needed to elect "sergeants-at-arms," which we did–and that helped greatly at the next meeting. The fact still remains, we come together, albeit in the name of the Lord, with many problems in our lives. And that is ok. That is why we are here. If we stay together and work and struggle together, we can be changed and we can grow. None of us really know the depth of what it means to let Jesus be Lord of our lives—but those who want can grow into it, into ourselves as "new creations." But for us who are part of the co-op, there is definitely struggle involved in that growth.

For example, our previous Steering Committee was adamant about making a rule to deal with those who come to meetings under the influence of drugs or alcohol. They did make a rule. Well, the very first person to whom we had to apply the rule was a member of the Steering Committee who had been quite vocal about the need for the rule and how obvious it would be when we needed to apply it. He wasn't happy! Denied that he was really under the influence—claimed he had only taken what his doctor ordered! To his credit he came around, and made a public apology in the co-op meeting. [We can't make rules from which a few of us are exempt just because we've been elected something or other (though it is the norm in our society, it seems)!]

But it is all such fun. I love the work.

So, now, how do we move into this self-development? We began by agreeing we can't form any other kinds of business or anything else if we can't trust each other. So, self-development forces inward searching immediately, even before we can do any outward projects. But how we grow spiritually and whether we can form viable projects, we are totally dependent on the Lord. Totally. The *Lord* will have to make this "go."

And that, too, makes it fun. Otherwise, I'd be *carrying* this co-op on my back, thinking I need to make it go (I've certainly done that a lot). And that's no fun at all.

Thank you again for your loving support.


Easter, 1992

Dear Friends and Relatives:

A member of the co-op just called. He was told yesterday that his belongings would be put on the street tomorrow unless he comes up with $180. How is he going to get $180 on two days' notice? He gets $110 in food stamps each month—that is it! He lives on that. How does he do it? Creatively, sparsely—not living very well. But he was rooming with someone, and that someone took part of his food stamps for rent. But at the beginning of last week, that person, who was also his best friend (and safety net), was killed when struck by an automobile. My co-op member's name is not on the rental contract. Can he be kicked out without a warrant or eviction notice? I expect so, but don't know for sure—I have made two calls to lawyers, but don't know yet. Anyway, he came to the church; he came to his co-op friends. He knew he had someone to go to—certainly for respect and prayer, perhaps to help work it out, perhaps for money. But, $180 is a lot of money for the church on short notice, too. Lord, work this out please. Give the guidance and wisdom needed.

We don't have many resources here. I heard a nationally known preacher say that a recent New York Times article claims that now 1% of the population owns 90% of the wealth of our country. Can that be true? My folks in the co-op feel like it is. They have the least. The March 1992, "Bread for the World" newsletter reports that 5.5 million children in our country are actually hungry, while another 6 million do not have enough to eat. The 5.5 million is 1 in 5 children. (Also, among industrialized nations America now ranks 21st in infant mortality rates.) Meanwhile, a smaller percentage of the population gets a bigger piece of the pie, and down here, our piece is woefully small and keeps getting sliced thinner. My co-op people are among those who have the hungry children.

And my friend who doesn't want to be evicted? Well, he doesn't want to live there either. Someone else in the house keeps stealing his stuff. He can't bring "home" his co-op food and leave it, or anything of value, because a guy on dope who also rooms in the house keeps breaking in and getting his stuff. However, his choices are limited. He can't afford to be on his own and he is crippled from an on-the-job accident, which limits his ability to get work.

My people live in some awful places. They don't want to be in them; but then they don't want to be out of them.

So many of the choices are hard. Pushing around peanuts is all it amounts to. You don't have to live here long to see why people are so depressed and feel trapped, why they turn to something—drugs, alcohol, sex, violence—to numb themselves. The fear, the worry, the hopelessness, the anger—they are strong. Can hope even be born in such circumstances?

I pray so. I know the resurrection only comes where there is actual death. There is death here.

Come, Holy Spirit; come, Lord Jesus.


June 1992

Dear Friends and Relatives:

Yesterday I had the privilege of going to court to

support one of our co-op members. I didn't even know she was in jail, but two other members told me she had been in there more than a week. She was without her epilepsy medicine, which the police refused to accept from her friends, plus she went through DTs during this jail stay. She really had a very rough time—very probably life threatening, with the epilepsy-alcohol mix.

Honestly, I had so much work to do—I had not envisioned spending time at the court—and it *always* turns out longer than you think it will be. But I knew she needed support and had the sense I was doing the right thing, that somehow the Lord would use my presence. I found the right courtroom and sat there for a long time. I had to go put more money in my parking meter, then more waiting. Her boyfriend was there which gave me a chance to get to know him better (though "no talking" in the courtroom). I saw my accused friend brought into the waiting area, but once she sat down she could not see us nor we her—the bottom of the glass is painted black so prisoners cannot see out. For all she knew she was alone.

After more time yet, two men came into the courtroom. I knew one of them—a Christian lawyer who defends indigent people. He saw me and came over. When he found out why I was there, he offered to represent her on the spot, got the citations from the clerk, and stood with her. One charge was dismissed, the other she pleaded *nolo contendre* (no contest) and it was accepted and she was allowed to go free, based on time already served. That was the Lord at work, demonstrating to my friend, who has no standing whatsoever in the world, that the Lord knows her and loves her. And she knew it, too. Also, it makes all the difference in the world when someone can "be there." I was able to be there—if I had not been, my lawyer friend would never have known and stood with her—she would have had no advocate—though just knowing her friend and I were there obviously heartened her once she saw us. She's desiring to be free of the alcohol—she knows she had a close call. She's not a "bad" person and did not need to be placed in jail longer. It's a joy to see the Lord use our co-op togetherness to draw people closer to him.

A short note on a different subject, namely

development aspects of the co-op. Hardly anybody in our co-op has a car (and those are old and rickety, needing constant work, often uninsured for lack of funds, etc.). Our co-op is a "4th world" people, as some now say—a world without cars (among other things) placed in a world of abundance where everything is far away. Well, anyone who wants to get out to a good grocery store, with fair prices and a good selection of foods, pays someone who has a car anywhere from $5 to $15 for a ride. We are looking at the possibility of getting a van to enable us to shop less expensively. Pray with us about it, as there are many obstacles to overcome: money, where to keep it safe from vandalism, etc.

Thank you for the various ways you support us.

## July 1992

Dear Friends and Relatives:

A few days ago, one of the members of the Steering Committee came with her friend to see me. He needed some clothes. I know him, though not well. But I could not tell who he was when he came in.

Three weeks earlier one of his "friends," a guy with whom he hangs around some, had beat him with a bat. I knew Arthur had been in the hospital, but I didn't know why—now I knew. Here it was almost a month later and the man was unrecognizable: face swollen, eyes nearly shut. The medical people had had to do reconstructive work on his face. I don't know how he is still alive, and don't know whether there might be any lasting brain damage. This man was beaten badly.

I asked Arthur how this happened. He didn't give too much of an answer. He most likely doesn't know—with being unconscious and under the influence of something— alcoholic and using drugs, too. What a killer! Addiction— we are overcome with it here. It is a "power" (as in Paul's "principalities and powers") for sure in our area: a demonic force that takes lives and creates and maintains social chaos. Most likely, his "friend" is addicted, too. I prayed with them that God might use this awfulness to break the addiction and free Arthur to new life. (There is some greater hope because of being able to minister to someone at such a moment—but as of now Arthur shows no real sign of realizing his predicament.)

At our first co-op meeting of July, so many of us were obviously under the influence (about 6 or so), the Steering Committee decided we couldn't ignore our rule— if a person is intoxicated, he or she cannot get food that day, but must return for it. Unfortunately, we had not been keeping the rule strictly so when we decided to enforce it, a wild scene ensued of drunk people defending themselves, having no clue that their behavior was abominable and a large part of the issue: crying, shouting, one woman threatening to use a razor against our president (whom they elected, and the rule is one we all voted on—proposed by one of those who was drunk!). "Never, I'm not coming back here!" (shouted repeatedly by one person); "I'm out of here—you won't see me again!" But they all returned sober and quietly the next day to pick up their food.

Gerald May in his book *Addiction and Grace* writes that "addiction is the most powerful psychic enemy of humanity's desire for God"(p.3). His opinion is that "all of us suffer from addictions"(p.3) but that the most tragically addicted people are those addicted to narcotics and alcohol (p.5). Having my own addictions keeps me from being so judgmental, but the drug and alcohol addictions are maddening, saddening, discouraging.

May seems to be saying, too, though, that addiction is a misguided, distorted desire for God. If that is so, then we certainly have "potential" here! Pray with us for God's grace to break in with recovery and resurrection life. We are seeing signs of it happening—and there will be more. (I have permission to write about Arthur.)


September 1992


Dear Friends and Relatives:

The Lord has been good to us and has sustained us these months since I first wrote to you. In the co-op we are able to buy food and basically keep up our obligations in the church building. And our God has given daily bread to us as a family. I thank you for your part in that.

But right at the moment, the finances are problematic. And while I know that my job, according to the scriptures, is to seek first the kingdom and not to be anxious, I am anxious. It is tricky to write about this, but I am not writing to ask you to do more—just continue to hold me in prayer that I will be faithful and learn from these slim times.

I beseech the Lord about all this financial stuff, and grow from the interchanges. I want it to be smooth sailing, but it is not. There are positive sides to it, one being that my empathy grows for my poor co-op sisters and brothers and their desperation and anxiety: how are we going to pay the rent, eat, get the heat back on with the cold approaching, etc.? These financial struggles draw us together—and it is touching to have the co-op members praying for me to make it financially, hoping we can continue to be together.

It is different to be in this society and be poor or identify with poor people. It is a strain, and I know it is one with which some of you identify, because you have let me know of your struggles. In a way, it is not a struggle I would choose, but on the other hand I know that it comes directly as a consequence of my choices, which I can honestly say have been about being faithful to the Lord as well as I could. My understanding of the Gospel has never let me be free of taking "the least of these" seriously. But when you do that, you can get somewhat displaced in our society.

I think of Moses—he grew up in the palace, but the Lord led him to be identified with the lowliest in the society. He changed places completely. As a man of God, he was alienated from the comfort that was his. I think of Abraham—called to a place that God would show him, having to leave what he knew, what was comfortable to him. Saul became Paul, moving from association with the persecutors to the "persecutees." Of course, our Lord left unbelievable privilege to be with us, to walk in our shoes. I have the daring to hope that my struggles have *some* relationship to this pattern, but then I see how timid, unloving and unfaithful I can be, and it is clear to me that I am no spiritual giant. And it doesn't *feel* very godly, this place—rather, I feel uneasy and anxious about how we will make it. (Yet I know the Lord has not forgotten me.) In any case, as I said, all this helps me know—not just know—feel—some of the terrible pressures of those who are at the bottom of our society. And I learn things from this vantage about myself and society that I can't learn from comfort. Finally, it pushes me to more deeply depend on—and wrestle with—our Lord, which, regardless how uneasy I am, I am certain is movement in the right direction.

## January 1993

Dear Friends and Relatives:

A number of you have said that you enjoy this newsletter. I have appreciated your comments (though I am not at the point of having a "letters-to-the-editor" section). I hope through this means to give you a somewhat accurate picture of what is going on with me and the co-op.

John Arnold will visit the co-op and speak with us tomorrow. John works with the state extension services teaching about the value and possibilities of urban gardening. One of our members has a large plot of land behind her house, which her landlord owns and says we can use. I am hopeful that there may really be genuine interest among our members for pursuing this, as it will be a healthy and inexpensive way to obtain food and to work together. But ... I have long since learned not to count chickens before they hatch. We will see.

The daughter and sister of some of our co-op members had a baby. Like many, the babe was premature, underweight, addicted—the poor child had to come into the world suffering from underdevelopment and having to withdraw from drugs. The mother's life is a wreck but she always smiles and avoids serious talk whenever I see her. So, I wanted to visit her at the hospital, for such a moment is a uniquely pastoral one that I should not let pass. And, though hesitant, she was actually longing to talk about the matters that weigh on her heart, the guilt that this child is addicted and that her one-year old is underweight and not eating right, knowing that she is responsible. It was not long before she was crying (trying *not* to cry). I offered my handkerchief. She wanted to be "strong enough" to resist the drugs most of her family pushes on her, and it was hard for her to consider that she is not strong enough on her own. Of course, her resolve was strong then, away from the family and seeing the consequences of her actions, but that will shortly be eroded. She prayed, asking for forgiveness and the grace to be the mother she longs to be; then she asked to keep my handkerchief "for a souvenir." Was this little visit remarkable to her? We did talk, we did pray, and she knows I cared enough to come.

It is a step. And God is good. Again, we will see.

February 1993

Dear Friends and Relatives:

I continue to be aware of the violence that is part of the life of the co-op members. And consequently, I'm more aware of the importance of coming together for support and respite.

Sabrina got someone to call us from the Grady Hospital emergency room Thursday—she had been beat up by four guys at her apartment complex. A courageous bus driver stopped them as they were trying to pull her toward a wooded area.

When the Steering Committee met, Deborah was late, because as she left to head to the meeting, she went out to find an elderly lady just having been left by thugs. She got the help she needed and stayed with her a while. This precipitated a number of reports of various ways people had been accosted—children's shoes taken at gunpoint, etc.

Rudine wanted us to pray because her grandson, who is 21, had been shot. He was lucky—his knee is shattered, but the gunman tried to fire again at him only to have the gun click.

One of the persons who was absent from the Steering Committee meeting called me later to say she stayed home because she was keeping the children of her best friend, whose husband had been killed while at work by a gunman who came into the place and started shooting.

While we met, someone came into the church and

went into the kitchen where lunch was being prepared for the daycare children and took all the meat set out to thaw while the two kitchen workers had gone back to the activity rooms.

A woman I know who lives four blocks from here has taken much interest in the teen-age boys, and spends some time teaching them. Of the ten she started with last year, three are now dead. Her own son was stabbed in the neck by another boy, though not fatally. (She constantly prays and cares for him, and the doctors say his ability to walk is a miracle. He still has trouble—but she is not through praying!)

Saturday night the church was broken into again. Almost think I'd be better off not locking my office door— more torn up but keeps no one out. Don't have anything of value to be taken—once again, my heater's gone, things strewn around. It does get old, though.

Most of us do not have to live in such a climate, I am glad to say. But in such an alien and unfriendly place, the co-op and the community ministry are sources of comfort and solace to people. We can talk about these things, pray together and strengthen one another and remind each other of what is important. It helps to talk, cry and grieve together, call upon the Lord together. Because we gather in God's name, there is a place to bring these matters, to lament. We can gather around the food, which is a gift, and we are in an oasis. Together we can make it, and together we can pray—for those victimized, for those who perpetrate such things, for one another.

It's important to be here. It's a good place to be. I pray the Lord will keep us safe, but more importantly, keep us faithful.


March 1993

Dear Friends and Relatives:

On March 4 we had our 2nd anniversary celebration for the food co-op. The members did nearly all the work with the steering committee doing most of the planning. It was a proud moment for our members.

A group was supposed to come sing for us, but they did not. So, several of the co-op members and visitors formed a quartet and sang while we ate. We have some talent we didn't know was present among us. Do I see a choir in our future?

The meal was prepared by the co-op members, Jackie Palmer in charge. They arrived early—about 7:30—to begin their preparations, and they did well. Deborah McReynolds baked a cake that was part of the gift to the food bank for their role in our having food, and she brought it on the bus from her home!

Kathy Palumbo of the Atlanta Community Food Bank spoke to us about the need for those who are in the co-op to speak out in relation to legislation and other issues that affect them. It was a good word for us, as we had talked about writing congressional representatives, etc., but had not followed up in any way.

We made use of the event to thank the Lord and many people who have helped us. And I thank you again for your part in keeping us going.

The new Steering Committee is just taking hold and I am excited about the future. Given her history, our new president, Lucille Posey, seems like the most unlikely of candidates for this job. I've mentioned her before—about three years ago I remember asking Lucille whether she might consider treatment for her alcoholism. She wasn't interested—she didn't want to stop drinking! But today she has been sober for about a year and is the president of the co-op! This is a new kind of responsibility for Lucille, but it's appearing as though she may handle it quite well. She loves it, and though she is very quiet, she is willing to work.

Rudine Cook, our new vice-president, is assuming the responsibilities of her new job in an admirable way also. She has been sober for a good while, too. She and Lucille are looking like a good team. Neither of them has cars but they have walked to visit the steering committee members who were not present at the last meeting. The three of us met early before the last co-op meeting, as both want to learn how to lead meetings and to plan the meeting's agenda. It's great to have committee members who desire to learn and grow, and to see the Lord work in such wonderful ways in the lives of these people is a great joy. It makes up for many frustrations. I do believe the Lord is using this co-op to promote life!

We have also found an organization that is willing to do some leadership training with our steering committee and they plan to pursue it. More life! And it is looking like the garden may pan out—the soil test was quite positive and about ten members show real interest. A workday is planned for Mar. 31. New life here, too! The Lord is good.

May 1993

Dear Friends and Relatives:

John Luther, my youngest child, is 5. He helps me with my newsletter (at times). If your letters appear kind of wrinkled, folded funny, glued too much, John's your man! Any letters to the editor about these matters will be directed to his department.

Let me introduce you to one of the food co-op members. Sarah came by today when we were ending our steering committee meeting. I was glad she came; she was in danger of being suspended from the co-op, as she had not been keeping in contact nor coming to meetings (turns out she had been in the hospital).

Sarah is a dear. She lives in a house which, like a number of houses in the area, is an urban version of a rural sharecropper shack: cinderblock outside and inside—no sheetrock, plaster, no nothing on the walls, pale green, plain looking, drab and uninviting. The whole house is tiny, but it is a duplex and she lives in one-half of it. It is a struggle for her to get by—her phone has been cut off "temporarily." Being out of food, she had come to the church for a food voucher.

Last year for several months she cooked for anyone who wanted to come to her house for breakfast—at no charge. She got up at 4 a.m. to get ready. She fed up to 80 people in her house every morning! But she couldn't pay the bill, so she's had to stop. The children concern her the most: "I just can't stand to see children hongry (sic)." She'd like to start again, but so far that is not working out. I've wondered if or how the co-op might help. She is trusting that God will make a way. Sarah is 86, I think.

Our leadership training sessions have gone well. They definitely get our steering committee members talking together. I hope the members will move toward taking more responsibility and authority. There are indications of that happening: one steering committee member said to me in a meeting, "Nothing gets done around here if *you* don't want it done." Ouch! –and Hallelujah! Thank God for someone who will stand up and speak. That's movement toward the members taking more ownership. As it stands, I can hold onto too much power. Clearly, I don't always find a right balance between being an "advisor" to the co-op and making sure things get done, which keeps people dependent on me. It appears the leadership training is being used of God to shift the balance.

The garden group seems to be doing well. It is its own entity within the community ministry, with its own elected officers. I don't have a plot, but I've worked up there a couple of days—you'd think we had thrown out glass seed, there is so much broken glass in the ground. But things are growing—friendship, tomatoes, beans, awareness of God's creation....

The enclosed brochure may go a ways toward giving us an air of respectability. We got it ready in time for the benefit concert (which, by the way, went well, though it was small. We raised $750, which is very helpful and will enable us to live to ride another day). If you know of someone who might have an interest, pass it on, as the financial scene continues to provide day-by-day drama.

June 1993

Dear Friends and Relatives:

Theft. Again. Of the 23 one and a half pound packages of chicken set aside for co-op members who would be coming later for their food, 16 were stolen—by people in or related to the co-op! There were few enough people present, and there were people who saw what happened, so we know something about this. Even so, getting at what really transpired is very difficult.

When members come into the co-op, each takes a pledge. It reads, "I pledge to be a faithful member of the Georgia Avenue Food Cooperative with the help of God. I will uphold the guidelines and ask that others help hold me to them. I will work to make the co-op successful and will respect the staff and members of the co-op. I will not gossip about anyone in the co-op and will endeavor to learn to 'speak the truth in love' to those with whom I have disagreements."

Well, the whole brouhaha raised by this theft rakes the co-op member's pledge through the coals. Obviously, stealing from others is not making for success. Plus, there has been much gossip, people have lied, and when the truth has been spoken it has not been in love. Clearly, there is not much respect being demonstrated. Our Steering Committee has been working on this now for several weeks, and there is much still up in the air.

Now, I'm not glad that some of our members have stolen; but as I see it, the food co-op is a large net in which to gather those whose way of life may include lying, stealing, gossiping, etc., yet most of whom claim to follow Christ. The co-op wasn't started with the idea that we would only accept perfect people—quite the opposite. We want anyone who can take our pledge—including the "worst"— to enter this field of training so we can grow together and take our professed discipleship seriously.

Of course, addressing this theft starts out with certain rancor in our hearts, finger pointing, the drive to oust the offenders—in short, not with compassion for the perpetrators, but with vengeance and a little self-righteousness. But I pray we will love these newfound chicken-thief "enemies" even as we confront, not overlook, all that has happened. If we are willing to see it, we will recognize that none of us is innocent. As the "advisor," a large part of my job is to remind us all of the pledge we took, to "keep us in the ring." Our pledge then functions to hedge us about, words that were perhaps empty when we said them gain power, and just maybe we will end up examining ourselves, not just accusing others.

The point of all this is that the chicken theft is a great

opportunity. While immediately unsettled, a certain part of me soon smiles when such an incident occurs: ah yes, this will definitely stir the pot. Come and guide us, Holy Spirit. Convert our hearts. Form new community.

The garden is going well. It is now an entry in an urban garden contest that will be coming up next month. Go garden!

I do want to thank you again—for a number of you send your money, which helps keep us going. I am grateful for your support and for your trust.


## July 1993

Dear Friends and Relatives:

In 1984, I visited Big Hawk in jail. I didn't know him: his mentally challenged daughter, who attends the church faithfully, asked me to visit her father in prison. The visit turned out to be an incredible turning point onto a wonderful/terrible new path for him, and in some ways, me.

Hawk said that he was a major drug mover in the city, having begun his "trade" right after the Korean War. At the time I met him, he still owned four lots together, with two houses, a Cadillac limousine, and a van, and had a number of apartments with women, two of whom I've met, whom Hawk tells me bore him a total of 23 children. His life could not have been more different from mine, so that I sometimes found myself unsure what was the truth about what he said.

As I say, as a result of that visit, Big Hawk changed. He did not become a model citizen, but made a basic turn toward God and left the drug money and life behind. It has been unbelievably hard for him. The pressures to turn back to the old way have been tremendous: he went from being a drug kingpin to shining shoes downtown, to being completely broke with no vehicle or home. His wife and most of his family were in a rage at him for no longer providing the good life, and of course, instead of being part of the family of a big shot, they became part of the family of a fool who all of a sudden was talking about God and trying to convert them. The change in Hawk was hard for just about everybody. People in the church couldn't believe he really had changed so, and the people that did know him well couldn't believe he had changed so. He was a man without friends. And he thought he would move from being "Big Hawk" in the neighborhood and drug world, with all his authority, to being Big Hawk in the kingdom of God (which alienated everybody). But of course, it doesn't work that way. So Big Hawk has been broken down and dismantled by the Spirit, little by little, piece by piece, over these last 9 years.

I am thinking about Hawk because a month ago he had a stroke and can hardly talk. He is recovering, no longer puffed up with himself, but an old man who is humble and full of joy and thanksgiving to God. He is now living in an efficiency apartment of the Atlanta Housing Authority. You would have thought when he moved in with the used furniture we got him that he had moved into a palace. He had been virtually homeless, unable to be around his addicted wife, and when he finally got his own place in a nearby high rise, he was full of rejoicing. He said he finally could pray and be quiet before the Lord in peace—and also finally sleep!

It has been painful to be close to Hawk. The Lord put us together—God knew Hawk needed someone knit to him or he would not make it, and so he joined Hawk and me together. We love one another—it's just there, a given. I can't remove it. Hawk has hurt me—in one of his lowest moments, he stole ("borrowed" for an extended period) my car, and many people, including many who were close to me, felt I was a fool to stick with him. I might have been—I wondered, too, but I was doing the best I could at the time, and, as I said, I love him, and you will do things that are hard to understand for someone you love. But I always believed he genuinely turned to God—even when it seemed otherwise. And I always knew he was under mind-bending pressure.

Now Hawk has a new sense of community and love within the church. It has been long coming. Hawk has paid a price for all his evil: he's always saying, "I'm a living witness that you reap what you sow—you can't plant corn and reap watermelons." But he says it with wonder and tears at the grace of a God who would give him something even better than watermelon, love even one as evil as he had been, one who says he was "a general in the devil's army."

I wouldn't go back and ask the Lord to "unknit" me from Hawk. Being a witness and participant in this powerful resurrection has been a privilege. I am grateful to be here.

August 1993

Dear Friends and Relatives:

Fay was raised here, "in the streets," so she has great potential to minister to others here. She had a hard time— her father was mostly gone, being in jail. When she came to Georgia Avenue Church, she was a judgmental charismatic, her life was in shambles, and she was married to an alcoholic who abused her. That was more than 10 years ago.

Over those ten years, Fay has indeed become a wonderful, loving minister to her neighbors and the people whom we serve in the community ministry. She is herself a member of the food co-op, but she is also a minister with me in the community ministry. Fay's gifts of prayer and faith, her generosity amidst poverty and deep love for all have been such a blessing to me.

Our church has been using the season of Pentecost for individuals within the church to speak from the pulpit about how the Holy Spirit has guided, changed, influenced their lives. Fay spoke and it was beautiful: it became clear listening to her that the one who was last has become first— the one who-came-from-the-streets has surpassed us middle-class-ones with all our answers in her loving acceptance of people, no matter how low or how smelly. Fay often gives me credit for being used of God to help bring her to a new place—but I have to say, in many respects, the pupil has surpassed the teacher.

Financially, Fay survives on very little. She refuses to be in the welfare system, and she knew that if she took a regular job, she would have to be away from her three children, which she was not willing to do. Children need their mothers in this environment (in any environment), since the temptations and threats are many for young ones—they need a guiding hand to be there with them at all times. Fay made a good choice, even though it has made it very hard financially. She has had great faith and trusted God that she was doing the right thing and the Lord should provide. He has—and she has led us by her faith.

And Fay has raised her children well. Her eldest child is 18 and has a full scholarship for books and tuition to a local college. Yet, Fay had prayed with me for more—that the Lord would provide a way for him to live away from home!

And the Lord has answered. I was privileged to go with Fay and her son to visit a businesswoman who said she wanted to help someone with college. We had to drive a ways out to the scary suburbs, but we had a wonderful visit. This Methodist woman said she had been blessed financially and wanted to help others, and she graciously "adopted" Pancho, offering to pay his living expenses so he could concentrate on school and leave home. It was a beautiful moment—we all ended up crying together—and what joy to see those two mothers connect, though some miles and many dollars apart. So, we will see how Pancho does, but Fay's prayers and faithfulness have been answered, and just maybe Pancho, too, will someday minister here in his own way as one who understands these urban streets.

Your prayers and financial support help keep the various facets of our ministry going. I am grateful to you.


September 1993


Dear Friends and Relatives:

We began our Wednesday worship service and lunch program again after breaking for the summer. During the summer, we need the building space for other programs—children's programs and such. I always feel some excitement about beginning anew in the fall. Truthfully, it is a shame that we have to have such a program, but I enjoy it. I don't like the brokenness I see; I don't like seeing the results of the long years of sinful oppression begun with slavery and the willingness of some of us to use certain people and define them as less than human. We and they, the nation, all of us, have reaped and are reaping terrible consequences of our inhumanity. Lord Acton's famous statement "power corrupts, and absolute power corrupts absolutely" and it's corollary "powerlessness corrupts, and absolute powerlessness corrupts absolutely" are mirrored in the lives of those of us who gather. Yet I always like those meals together.

People bring their needs and hurts to our gathering. One man needed a pair of socks—his feet were getting eaten up by mosquitoes as he sleeps outdoors wherever he can... a homeless woman asked us to pray with her for a place to live, and someone else in the room offered her temporary space. That prayer was answered quickly. A man wanted prayer because he had shot someone with a sawed-off shotgun: some people had plotted to kill him and though he acted out of self-defense and the police exonerated him while the plotters have been arrested, he wanted prayer because it weighs on his mind. And we celebrated the birth of a 19-year old's 1 lb., 7 oz. girl—the doctors said she wouldn't live an hour. We had prayed, asking the Lord to make a way for the little one, and the tiny lady has made 3 days now.[1]

A number of people come to the worship service we hold beforehand. People are not required to come to the service in order to join in the meal—we are not trying to force our faith on anyone. The worship service is an invitation; the meal a gift. Also, anyone can eat—rich or poor. Last year, when I was unable to be there at one point because of my back trouble, one of the servers from another church told someone that didn't look poor they shouldn't eat, since the food was only for people in need. Ouch! That's not hospitality, and that is not our stance—anyone can eat who will join in. That way we have fellowship that transcends our economic definitions; and anyway, we don't

---

[1] As of this publication, this little bitty baby is a thriving adult.

want to make people feel that much more separated because of being "needy." It's hard enough as it is for some folks to have to join in such a meal, though we greet people warmly and let them know of our joy at seeing them. In the scriptures, meals were often moments in which the Lord revealed his presence. And the Master of the universe appears here, too, not only as the Holy Spirit, but in the varied faces which gather to sit at the table... faces of races, classes, mixed motives, the genuinely humble and deceptively conniving, addicts, prostitutes ... we break bread together, awaiting a yet greater banquet.


December 1993


Dear Friends and Relatives:

Christmas provokes me to stop to reflect on the ways the Lord has blessed me. They are so many. My wife and our children are a great gift to me, and I am so thankful to be with them. Barbara has a wealth of remembrances and energy for Christmas, which certainly make life for John and Helen and me much richer. Our tree is beautiful, laden with ornaments, some of which go back for her family as far as the Depression era. And it is such a joy to share the mysteries of this time with little ones: Helen at 9 and John at 6 help capture a sense of magic about the season.

Georgia Avenue Church is a great gift to me. We are pretty small, 30 or so folks. The Lord has brought us through so much together that we now begin to approach being a family. I am very grateful to have such good people around me. Over the last several years, we have worked together at developing Advent as a worship season. We decorate the sanctuary beautifully, and our Advent worship times and gatherings have a special joy about them; our Worship Committee does a good job with them. At Advent, I am especially aware of God's graciousness when we gather from such different backgrounds in wonderful moments of unity in praise of such a loving Creator.

The Wednesday noon folks and the co-op members are also such a blessing in my life. For some reason, I keep thinking of this one person in the co-op who makes me laugh, and my enjoyment of him is a gift to me. What helps to make him funny now, though, is not funny. Several years ago, someone came into his room while he was asleep and hit him in the head with an ax. That he is alive is amazing— he spent nearly a year in the hospital having reconstruction done on his head. He lost one eye. But he is such a character now and he knows in a slow, kind of innocent way, that he is funny. He generally wears a cap that is like an old flying cap, a Snoopy cap with flaps that pull down over his ears that can snap under but which he usually leaves hanging loose. With that cap on and with his long face, often-runny nose, and oversized glass eye, he presents quite a picture.

But this one incident in particular cracks me up: he came in one day to show me his new, smaller, eyeball. He decided he needed to clean it as he had been instructed, but as he proceeded to take it out, lo and behold, he dropped it! Of course, we searched high and low for his eyeball, which we found, to our great relief, in his cap, which he had had upside down on his lap when he took the eye out. But every time I picture him and think of him taking his eye out and dropping it, I almost laugh. The people of the community ministry gift me with laughter and tears as I get to know them and their struggles against some terrible odds.

At Christmas time, I am aware that God has blessed me and us all very much, most especially with the Lord's own presence among us. May a sense of God's lavish goodness bring you great joy now and in the New Year.

February 1994

Dear Friends and Relatives:

For the first time, and I hope for the last, we have lost a whole family from the food co-op. As I was sending out the last newsletter, I got a call that a family of three died of asphyxiation in their apartment because of gas leaks and vents that were clogged. Josephine Ricks and her son, Ronnie, were regular attendees of the co-op and the Wednesday noon meetings; the father stayed home because of blindness and health problems. They have been coming to our meetings for most of our years.

I think I have seldom known a poorer family. It's not that they had no money at all—they were just poor: meek, unobtrusive, plodding, walking everywhere, wearing the same old coats, not bothering anyone, quiet, keeping to themselves, not asking for favors except in cases of real need, not knowing how to use the resources available, seemingly devoid of ego, having no knowledge of what was going on around them or caring. Something about them made me think of pictures of eastern European refugees. Josephine was friendly if spoken to and Ronnie could be positively outgoing at times.

And true to form, they had no influence. My understanding is that they had talked to their landlord about the vents and the gas company about the leaks. But nothing was done. The only influence poor people have at times is when their suffering is so great it penetrates our insulation and cold-heartedness. In the Ricks' case, it is too late in this world. I will miss them.

When I took Hawk his co-op food after the last meeting (he often cannot get out now), a little girl came in to see him. Actually, she was kind of tall, but acted quite young. She was cute and giggly and shy with a big smile that lit up her face and the room. Hawk introduced her as his youngest boy's girlfriend. She was there alone because the boy is in jail for having shot her. The boy says it was an accident, which is not at all clear—she said she wasn't wounded badly. She's pretty matter-of-fact about it all: this is her life, the circumstances with which she must deal. She says all the boys she knows have guns. We spent a little time talking; I invited her to come with Hawk to church. She joined with us to pray before I left. Hawk told me Sunday she was stopped after leaving his apartment and arrested for carrying a pistol. The boy is 14, she is 12.

I remind you of our third anniversary celebration, which will take place Friday, Mar. 11 at noon at the church building. Anyone who lives close by or will be in town is invited to join us. Please let us know by Monday the 7th by calling the church office at the number listed below.

Most of our people have been "out there" alone, not part of any larger community, their lives unknown and of "no 'count." In our togetherness there are at least hints of caring for one another, here people begin to be known and count, and families as poor as the Ricks can be remembered and honored. I am grateful I can live and work here.

## March 1994

Dear Friends and Relatives:

When we meet together as a food co-op on our Thursday food days, it can be so joyful. This week was like that. We got all the food together—we had two loads of bread brought by different people, we had rice and beans, and we had gotten a good bit from the food bank. You could feel the joy in the air: members working together to get food divided, unloading the truck, bagging the rice and beans amidst all the abundance.

It was exciting and fun. Not even a thought was given to the fact that most of the food was from the food bank and the breads were day old, taken off the shelf—only joyful thanksgiving that the Lord had provided.

After meetings, everyone takes off walking home with their food. Many members have shopping carts. (I don't ask where they've come from!) This last week, I took several of the folks home and in doing so I passed so many co-op members walking on various streets. I find it a joyful sight—I would that I had some vantage point in the sky and could see everyone fanning out at once, headed toward home with the food our Lord has provided.

I often feel there is a kind of "stone soup" effect that happens with us: we get together in poverty, because of need; but we end up with abundance in the moment. At our anniversary celebration, members of the co-op shopped, prepared, cooked and served all the food. Our "togetherness" allows us to pool our little bits of money, the $2.00 collected from members when we meet, so we were able to buy special foods and flowers for our serving table. A choir from a local elementary school came and sang for us—arranged by one of the co-op members whose child is in the school. What abundance! My goodness! Our cooks did a great job cooking greens and baking chicken, and with other foods that were supplied, we had a feast. We were prosperous and it was joyful.

At our banquet, we took the opportunity to thank some people who had been especially helpful to us, both from within and from outside the co-op. And this year we added something new—we gave awards to those who had been sober for a significant time and/or who had gone through an addiction program in order get sober. We encourage people to go to AA meetings (there are two held weekly in our building), but many do not, even though they are in fact staying sober, so they are not getting recognition anywhere for their achievements. Most of us need encouragement to keep going, and when we come together as we have in the co-op, we form a matrix in which there can be recognition, people can be valued, and then just maybe we can think new thoughts, think about our lives in new ways, realize for ourselves that we are needed and how much we are loved by God. At the co-op the next week, I was talking privately to one of the women, a mother, who is drinking so much, encouraging her to look at how she is killing herself and to take steps to break free. She said, "Next year I'm going to be up there—you're going to be giving me one of those awards." I pray so: my joy will be that much greater.

The Lord is good.

April 1994

Dear Friends and Relatives:

Calls. We get a lot of them from people needing financial assistance. Once the church had more money than we do now, and we were willing to be a source of assistance to the larger community whenever possible. Now we have very little money, and have decided the only people we can make an effort to assist are those actually connected with the church or community ministry. However, we can't seem to get off the referral lists. I have a suspicion that, since there are so few agencies available for referral, those who are besieged by calls refuse to let us get off their list. Whether we can fill needs or not, we are a name and number to whom they can pass people and thus get them off their own back; so, we keep getting the calls.

Sometimes it is hard to listen to the phone messages on the machine, especially after having been away for the day. Then there may be message after message of faceless voices asking, sometimes pleading, for help: "My son and I are going to be evicted today if we cannot come up with money by five o'clock...;" "Our lights have been turned off and we need $180 to get them back on...;" "My food stamps were stolen and me and my grandchildren don't have nothing in the house to eat...please call...."

Most often the voices are female—the women who have the children and are trying to keep a roof over their head, food on the table, utilities on. Single men sometimes get upset when they get turned down, and understandably—they get rejected over and over, because there is not enough to go around and the families with children are first priority.

And after taking the messages, of course, I must return the calls, because I feel bound to honor the caller, and say no, we can't help (though we are able to do a little with food at times). "Well, do you know anyone you can refer me to then?" is usually the next question. But they already have, in most cases, any number I can give them.

The needs are so great: so many living on the edge, falling over the edge, lost folks out there; folks living with constant anxiety, facing terrible choices. It was not meant to be this way, and should not. I sat with a young man whose mother was dying. Knowing his mother and her life and how his life had been with her, I wondered whether it would matter to him. But he was genuinely grieved, and he talked some about how hard it had been for her, such memories as times "Mama would go out and sell her body to put food in this boy's mouth." Have mercy! She is 44, going on 85, and has had an awful life.

Sometimes I sit by that phone list or think about the desperation of people and just weep; I can do so little. I cannot deal with the enormity of these burdens. I am not God, though I've tried to be. But God is God, and it is clear to me that the poor and the poor in spirit have a special place in God's heart, and to be in Christ is to be joined to them. My part is to offer what I can and to be open to the ways that being with my poor brothers and sisters makes me more human. As I see this happening, I know that my own "call" to serve in this place was God's mercy on me, for which I am grateful.


May 1994


Dear Friends and Relatives:

"Self-development" is a word I have often used in relation to the co-op; I have written to you about it as one of the important goals of our work in the community ministry. When I use that word, I am speaking of the ways those who are used to being recipients begin to give to others, to let their own talents and abilities and gifts come to the fore, the ways we learn to serve and care for one another as brothers and sisters. We have many expressions of this self-development already, probably the best being the elected Steering Committee, not only because it is freely elected by the members, but the committee itself puts in much extra time to make the co-op work, meeting between every co-op meeting and planning agendas, addressing problems, helping to take co-op collections, organize food distribution, plan for special events, etc. (And, of course, the co-ops are also an expression of self-development given that the members operate them.)

For the last three years, we have held conversations with any co-op members who wished to participate about putting together a proposal for a "self-development grant" offered by the Presbyterian (U.S.A.) denomination. Our co-op make-up exactly fits the criteria for the grant: poor women and women of color. Knowing about such resources and helping to link my people to them is part of my role. But for me these conversations have been rather exasperating: we were turned down the first year, and the next year we had endless and finally unproductive meetings which ended in scrapping what we talked about. This year, when I was about to give up that anyone would even be interested, two women came forward and said they would like to apply for a grant to start a second co-op. As I have mentioned many times, we have a waiting list (it is 112 families at last count), some of whom have been on the list for two years. These two women said they wanted to see these folks begin to obtain food. We spent time talking together, they ended up writing a handwritten 2-page proposal, and lo and behold, they have been awarded the grant! The grant will provide a modest stipend for each of them, pay for the food and miscellaneous needs of the co-op for one year.

The idea to start a 2nd co-op was entirely their idea, and it grew out of their concern for others who do not have enough food. It is touching to me to see this concern for their neighbors, and it clearly came from their hearts. I am grateful to the Presbyterian Church (U.S.A.) for making such an opportunity possible. This gives new depth and dimension to our prayers that those who are ministered to begin in turn to minister to their community.

This grant will affect changes in the community ministry; for these two women, who will have primary responsibility for the second co-op, this will be a new experience. No doubt these changes will bring many new demands, moments of crisis and growth for all of us; and suddenly I am aware of many unanswered questions! Bring 'em on! The Lord has made the new co-op possible in his own right time, and he will guide us day by day. (Such challenges are lots better than watching TV!!)


June 1994

Dear Friends and Relatives:

I do not say much in these letters about financial matters—in fact, several people keep telling me I say too little. And I am hesitant to say a lot. But if I am not giving out the information you need, just let me know. I am including a contribution envelope in this mailing for you who do not usually receive them, and I will try to remember to do that every so often (I always include one to those who send money monthly). Also, any check sent should be made to the Georgia Avenue Church and earmarked "community ministry."

One reason I do not say a great deal is that I think it

is more important to focus on the work and the people. A second is that a number of people are on this mailing list not because they requested to be, but because I put them on as a way to keep in touch somewhat. And I am very sensitive about having anyone think that I am hoping thereby to get them to make financial contributions. My stance is that if people wish to contribute freely, wonderful; I do not want anyone to make contributions otherwise. Either Lord Jesus will keep us going, or he will not, and then it is time for something else.

I do want those of you who have been making contributions large or small to know that I am so thankful to you. You do in fact enable me to continue here. We never quite meet our budget, yet we have come close enough to be able to keep going. It is very much a matter of daily bread, and over the months I have gotten more and more used to that and less anxious about whether we will make it. We are not a rich family in economic terms, as we have hardly any money in the bank, in fact are in some debt from not having raised enough to pay FICA[2] and IRS taxes last year. We live frugally, my wife Barbara being an excellent manager of our finances. But we have a nice home and the transportation we need and we eat every day. We do without certain things we would like, but that is part of the territory. The people who participate in our community ministry have less than I, of which I am conscious, and yet I am very appreciative of what we have. I take seriously our Lord's admonition to "seek first the Kingdom of God … and all else will be provided," and I endeavor to do that.

I do very much believe there is value in the work we are doing, and I also believe that without people who are people of goodwill addressing, in the ways they can, the racial and class divisions that beset us, our future is one that moves toward Yugoslavia or Rwanda, as we pull into our tribes and groups and classes. Our work isn't the most

---

[2] FICA stands for Federal Insurance Contribution Act, a tax to fund Social Security and Medicare programs. Pastors in the US are considered self-employed and must pay those costs from their salaries as they are not deducted by an employer.

dramatic or courageous that ever was, but I feel called to be here, and I pray that I will be faithful, and wiser and more creative as time passes. I am also conscious that the Lord must lead this work; my part is to follow that leading knowing that when the Lord leads, healing happens and our work grows in an organic, generally smooth manner.

Finally, please do not hold it against me if I do not write personal notes with my letter. I'm often running behind.


July 1994

Dear Friends and Relatives:

One particular member of the food co-op is intelligent and charming, but she can also be *volatile*! She is one of the members who obtained the grant to begin the new second food co-op.

At one of our co-op meetings about six weeks ago, she got into an argument with another member of the co-op. She was right about the particular issue—but the way she went about dealing with it was *much too strong!* She was yelling and she was loud. Being a large person, she is definitely an intimidating figure when she gets going like this. She just couldn't quit yelling despite the fact that others were trying to calm her. Everyone gets quite uncomfortable at these moments, especially since in this case the person she was yelling at didn't want to back down either.

Well, I didn't say too much right at that point, but I knew I needed to talk with her. After all, she was going to have real authority in the second co-op she is helping to organize and she could blow the whole thing away with an episode or two like that.

So, just after we got news of actually obtaining the money for the new co-op, I told her I wanted to talk with her. I went to her house and we sat on her little, dark, crowded front porch. I named what was on my mind about that incident, but really had barely begun to talk when she went off again: "If you're trying to tell me you don't want me in the co-op, you just say it! Don't beat around the bush with me. If you think I'm no good for the new co-op, say so..." and on and on. Once again, I couldn't get her to stop—she was like a train going down the track. I waved my arms, I said, "No, no, no—that's not it—just hold on—give me a chance to speak...." She finally quit raving and I said, "I'm not trying to get rid of you at all. That's not it—you know I like you...." I reminded her of our history together; then I talked about my concerns, and how she would have official influence in the new co-op, and she could really damage it. She listened and calmed down, realizing I wasn't trying to dump her or even condemn her. She said, "Yes, I know that's a problem I have—my temper. I've asked the Lord to help me with this...." I said I just needed to know from her how to work with her about it—what can I do when she is angry like that. She said, "I just need to go off somewhere when I'm like that." "Yes, but you may not remember—is there anything I can do right at that moment?" She invited me to speak to her and remind her that she needed to go outside and cool off. She said, "If you tell me that, I'll listen to you." That was what I needed to hear. We had a great talk, and she asked me to pray for her about it, and when I got ready, she stopped me and gave me a hug—that was the first time she ever did that.

Moments like that are worth a lot, but that wasn't the end of it. When we had our third planning meeting for the new co-op, she said that someone in the first co-op had accused her of just being in this for the money! She said that hurt her, and she started to go off again, and she stopped and remembered! She said, 'I calmed myself, and I told her, "You know we made announcements to get anyone who wanted to come to those self-development meetings—you could have come. Then I went to those meetings myself and I worked. But if you want to feel the way you do, then you can, but when I get back to my home, I'm going to pray for you." (And she told us, "And I meant it.") She told all this with a gleam—she knew she had not let her temper get the best of her and she had done the right thing. She also said she knew this woman and those with her were expecting her to go off, and they didn't know how to deal with this new person!

We celebrated. She knew she had acted differently. She had asked the Lord to make a shift in her, and it was so

(!) and she recognized it and was sort of amazed. It was gratifying. Hmmm! That was a moment to savor. We rejoiced together.


August 1994

Dear Friends and Relatives:

I have been surprised and thankful for the care being shown to us by a Sunday School class at the Second Ponce de Leon Baptist Church. The class has been most supportive, and twice now has asked me to speak to inform its members more about what we are doing. They have started their own fund to help with costs and others have sent money directly, and offered aid in other ways. It is most helpful and I am grateful.

Friday night our assistant shopper was robbed by four masked men with shotguns and large pistols. They came to her house, forced her and those with her to lie down on the floor, and then took all the money they had. She gave it to them, expecting to be killed, as robbers in a recent similar theft had had the woman lie down and then shot her in the head. We are very grateful she was spared. I have met with her in her home to pray and we spent time praying with her in our co-op meeting. Together we can begin bringing healing to our abused and traumatized sister.

We have now whittled our waiting list down by 60 and will contact a few more to get the 20 to 25 total for the new co-op. Since the earliest dated names on the list are from two years ago (that's much too long around here to expect to find many people at the same address), we just keep contacting folks down the list until we get enough responses.

When we do have the new member orientation meetings (we had one today), it is so much fun. I feel excited thinking about it. Today one of our new co-op coordinators led the meeting, and she did a *splendid* job. I didn't have to say a thing. Generally, I come to meetings expecting *anything*, being somewhat ready for the worst. I had hoped one of the co-op folks would train to take over that new member orientation function long ago; finally, it has happened.

When new people come to those meetings, I don't know what's really in their minds, whether they just come looking for the food or wanting something more. We go over our handout sheet word-for-word, spelling out purposes and guidelines and what members' responsibilities are. Everyone always wants to join. They get excited. I'm not sure why, but it is infectious. Perhaps it's a sense that we are doing something worthwhile, doing something about which we feel right and good. Of the four who came to today's orientation, none are church members, yet all of them were eager to join an organization formed in the name of the Lord. I can't wait for our first meeting on Sept. 9—I look for that to be a joyous time for our new members. I pray that our Lord will bless us to get off on the right foot. I remember the first meeting of the already established co-op—what a celebration that was! Not being used to shopping, we bought several hundred pounds too much food—but it was no accident: The Lord knew what he was doing to give us a great start. You are invited to the meeting: 11:30 a.m. at the church building. Call me if you need more information.

The Lord is so good. I'm not sure why all this gets me so stirred up. I think it is partly because it seems the smallest little things mean so much to people who have little and who are not used to being respected and welcomed and wanted. And it does touch me, I have to say.

September 1994

Dear Friends and Relatives:

We did get the second co-op started. It was and is good. Fay got up and got out to the food bank at 6 a.m. (in the midst of a storm!) to get us a good number so we'd have a good place in the shopping line. She got number 1(!), a good sign for our new co-op. Jackie did a fine job organizing the food distribution. We took loads of pictures and had a good time, celebrating and thanking the Lord for bringing this moment to pass.

I went to see the son of one of the co-op members.

He's in the Georgia Mental Health Center in a locked building because he's suicidal. A huge guy, he's depressed because he feels trapped in drugs; he can't keep a job and he can't buy the things for his son and his family that they need. But with the Lord there is hope. It seemed to me there was a lot to the guy (beyond size) and I was impressed with how much he was concerned about others on the unit whom he felt were not really getting the care they need from the staff. When I was leaving, a young man who very obviously had mental problems took me by the hand and started leading me off. We sat down in the floor at the end of the hall—he handed me a Bible and made sounds indicating he wanted me to read. I did and we prayed. When I left, I asked the big fellow to keep spending time reading with him and praying: he needs to be ministering to someone and the young fellow needed to be ministered to. They were both tickled with the arrangement.

When I picked up the co-op treasurer for the steering committee meeting, I was noting that most of the houses around her are vacant. It really looks like hell—trash in the uncut shrubbery, overturned beds, etc. It's no place to be raising children. But her other options are worse. Lord, please...!

Duke came late for his co-op box. He mentioned that he had worked for the labor pool Saturday night washing dishes at a hotel, 11 p.m. to 8:30 a.m. He was paid $23.00! Since it was Sunday when he got paid, he had a hard time cashing the check they gave him—a restaurant charged him $3.00 to cash the $23.00 check. Let's see—$20.00 divided by 9.5 hours—just over $2.00/hr. He won't get out of poverty doing that work.

Hawk's wife Martha died. I was in Charleston and another member of the church who is also a pastor prepared to do the service. He was ready and waiting. When the family came in, another minister led them in and conducted the whole service. Hawk says he doesn't know who the man was, the funeral home says it doesn't know—nobody's owned up to contacting the man or knowing who he is. It's an interesting place to live.

Now Hawk tells me the insurance company says the policy he's paid faithfully for Martha won't be paid because it hasn't been two years since he started the "whole life" policy. Surely this is wrong—something more to check out. Folks here are determined to have insurance for their funerals, but I have seen several instances in which the insurance company had a "reason" *not* to pay the policy when the time came.

In many ways, poor people are vulnerable—"easy pickins!" I'm grateful you're concerned for these sisters and brothers.

October 1994

Dear Friends and Relatives:

Many of my poorer brothers and sisters here abhor the situation in which they find themselves, but to change it takes something *huge*—Herculean. It is impossible. A mother was referred to me, having thoughts of suicide. She has tried so hard, yet she sees herself losing her 16-year old son to the streets. He's skipping school; she has a job and can't keep up with him during the day and fears that he is getting into using or selling drugs despite all she's taught and done and threatened. She wants a home so badly to get out of the housing project, but must wait until non-profit housing gets around to her. Meanwhile, neighbors and relatives lean on her to give them this or that, even feed them, because she has a regular income, and she has a very difficult time saying no. The pressures weigh her down. She longs to have things better, but she is trapped by her race, the demands on her, her poverty, her lack of education. There is no easy solution; no nice religious words I can say will make it all OK. She's ready to give up.

A recent "Baptist Peacemaker" newsletter reported about a young "Crips" gang leader named "Tony Bogard" Thomas who came to know the Lord and began to work in Watts Los Angeles to make a difference in his community, even making a truce with the "Bloods" gang to stop their warring. He was killed by gunfire January 14 of this year while raising money for a community project.

The young woman, who is a Christian, did give up: she gave up trying to take care of everything in her own strength, she placed her burdens in God's hands and reconnected with her faith. She left feeling much better. But she still lives in an inhuman situation; like Tony Bogard, she is not insulated from harsh realities. Some people live facing great odds.

I hear people make strong judgments about those who are poor. A recent *Atlanta Journal-Constitution* letter to the editor was particularly venomous in its denunciations of homeless "bums" and others, and I have heard radio talk show hosts, especially those from the conservative political spectrum, speak words I can only describe as hate toward people on welfare and poor people in general.

Poor people, like the rest of us, are not perfect. But those who make harsh judgments act as though they are worth more than poorer people and can take credit for being in better circumstances. Yet none of us chose to whom we would be born nor the circumstances thereof; we did not choose the abilities that would be innate to us. We found ourselves in our situation, and we did well or not according to some strengths or weaknesses for which we also cannot take credit. Even if we had the wits to become millionaires, we cannot take credit for those wits or being in an environment where wealth was possible.

The Bible reverses our judgments: in the story of Lazarus and the rich man (Lk.16:19-31) the rich man who was upright and religious stayed away from the filthy, unblessed bum, Lazarus, so he could be clean to keep the law. They both died: The godly rich man went to hell; the ungodly bum went to heaven.

December 1994

Dear Friends and Relatives:

One of the co-op members asked me to come to her house to pray with a neighbor whose daughter has AIDS. We walked together to the apartment of the neighbor. There, my co-op member introduced me to a woman named Carolyn, mother and grandmother, who took me into the living room where on a couch sat her daughter, a stick person, rigid, eyes bugged out, obviously dying. She now weighs 68 pounds and comes in and out of consciousness. She is Carolyn's only child, aged 22.

The daughter has had three children, the oldest of which is 7, the youngest 2. The middle child was born with AIDS and died from it at age 3. Carolyn had really cared for that baby, who died in May of last year. The other two little ones are dear (the youngest, a boy, has not thus far shown signs of the disease). The grandmother clearly loves them. She also clearly has her hands full with her only child an invalid, children, little food or money, no washing machine, car, etc.

I asked her if we could talk before we prayed. My co-op member had told me Carolyn had started drinking and was not handling things well. She certainly is one who needs strength and comfort, having so much grief and such a burden. She was glad for the chance to converse.

As we talked, I realized she was a rare person. She could send her daughter to a clinic where they would keep her, but Carolyn says she wants to take care of her only child whom she loves. She has a strong faith and is a regular church member and has pretty good support from her little church. They come pray with her, her pastor visits, and the family goes to church services as they are able. She told me a wonderful story about the child who died: She had told the little boy he had to live until she came back from surgery on her neck (she cannot move her neck and head freely because of fused bones). The child lived, but she realized she was holding on to him, so one day she prayed and put him in the Lord's hands because, though she did not want to lose him, she did not want the little one suffering. A few nights later, while asleep, someone shook her awake with strong motions. She tried to get her wits about her, opening her eyes to see who it was, only to see a bright light above her. She lay there wondering what this was, and she thought, "He's gone!" She went into the baby's room, and he was lying there with a peaceful look on his face with his eyes open, looking up as though toward someone who had reached out for him. He was gone: The Lord had come and comforted them both.

I did ask her about the drinking—she said she didn't overdo it—she couldn't because of the little ones. (I believed

54

her and said I'd be taking a drink now and then, too, if I had as much on me as she does.) I prayed with them and left.

This visit was a Christmas gift to me from my co-op member. I had met a saint and heard the story of the angel who came and gently took a child, at the season of the angel who came to announce a child. They were both the gracious work of God who is still "with us" and remembers the poor and lowly.


January 1995

Dear Friends and Relatives:

There is one vestige left from both my Texas roots and one-time interest in football: I still root for the Dallas Cowboys. Last Sunday they were playing a play-off game to get into the Super Bowl for the 3rd year in a row. I knew if they were going to win, they needed me to be watching the game and concentrating, otherwise they'd be fumbling and doing things that would hurt their chances.

But the only time I could visit this one man in this particular alcoholic treatment program was Sunday afternoon. Visiting hours started at 3:00—the game started at 4:00. Not too bad—I'd miss some of the game but get most of it.

I got to the place and was escorted to the visiting area, only to learn I had to sit through a *one-hour information class **before** I could visit!* Well… obviously a person is more important than a football game, so…. We finally got out of the class and had a chance to start talking. The man I was visiting began to tell me about this other fellow who was going to have to leave the program because his mother had just brought his little one-year old daughter to the campus and left her. The powers-that-be said, "Find a place for her *today* or leave today!" My friend wanted to know if I had a solution to the problem!

Well, no, I didn't have a solution to the problem. I knew I couldn't take the baby, and I didn't know anyone who could, on one hour's notice, take a baby for 4 to 6 months. (And who knew what the whole story was here anyway?)

And sure enough, up walked the man with the baby. He sat down and started talking—no, he didn't know what to do; the child's mother is a hopeless addict. There was one woman who had offered at one time to take care of the child, but he didn't know how to call her, and had no way to get there. This little baby was awfully cute; and this young man did need to stay in this program; and if he did leave with the child he was homeless anyway—he had nowhere to go! Of course, the game was getting under way by then, but my mouth opened on its own and I heard my voice say, "I'll take you to find this woman!"

It worked! We found her and she was glad to keep the baby!! As it turned out, the young man seemed to be a good person who really had been working at getting his life in order for himself and his child: he'd been attending a church, studying the scripture, and had checked himself into this program. It was great. He said he had prayed all day that the Lord would make a way for him to stay in the program, and the Lord had answered his request by sending me. I suppose he had.

On the other hand, it didn't help my team: since I wasn't there to watch, the Cowboys lost the game. I'm sorry, guys—I hope you won't be too sore at me.

We will have our food co-op's 4th Anniversary celebration lunch on Feb. 28. You are invited; we would love to have you join us. Let me know and we'll set a place for you. Plan to be here at the church building by noon.

February 1995

Dear Friends and Relatives:

When I sit down to write, often what comes to mind is the people with whom the Lord placed me to teach me, and occasionally be taught by me. And so it is this time.

One of our co-op members considers himself Muslim Baptist (I'll call him MB)—I've never met another Muslim Baptist. I don't think there are many of them out there. He's a Vietnam vet, quite crippled, though his condition is from an auto accident. He can walk with a cane, but his limp is severe. It's obvious his lower half is shriveled, while he is quite strong in the upper torso.

He was granted Social Security disability again recently. (He had it before, but was arrested after his father's death when his father's dog, which he had left in a neighbor's care during the funeral, bit someone. When he was arrested, his checks were stopped—this was more than a year ago, and he has had no income since. He tries to ply a trade of sign painting, but gets huge blisters on his hands and arms from his allergies to the paints.) Anyway, when it was restored, they sent him a lump sum check for something more than $5000. Since he is an alcoholic (he claims he is not addicted, but drinks because of the pain from his feet and hips), he has to have another person be the responsible payee. So he picked this fellow Hubert to get his check. As you might guess, much of the $5000 is gone and Hubert is not to be found. MB came to me asking me to be his payee.

We went to the social security office to sign my name on the line. I began to realize that MB was changing as we went along—he had been drinking before I picked him up at 10:30 a.m., which was not evident when he got in the car. But it became *very* evident as we waited in the social security waiting room. He got louder and more arrogant. When one of the social security workers stuck his head out the door, MB demanded *loudly,* "Yo! Hey you! I want to see you!" at which point the man disgustedly closed the door. I was glad when we could finally get out of there.

MB wanted to go to the Billy Graham Crusade when it was in Atlanta. So he and two other co-op members and I struck out. We were an interesting group: I was in my usual blue jeans, otherwise a fairly normal looking middle-class white guy; then there was MB, who is mulatto, dressed in military looking khakis, with a sort of Muslim-looking robe; he is a sight, with his leopard fez-like hat, unkempt beard, scarred, smash-nosed face and wild hair. There was also an African-American woman who has one stray eye and gold hair, and another white male, who has one crossed eye, has dyed his hair *very* black and had it combed *straight* down with oil of some kind on it. Overall, we reeked of tobacco smoke, plus a few other smells. We didn't fit in with the crowd at all, but in truth, I felt I was in good company.

We found seats easily enough. MB sat on the end of the row by the aisle as it gave room for his cane. He had not been drinking and was so enthusiastic about being there; happy as could be. He went right to sleep—I expect he was tired from being homeless right then. We kept having people turn around to look at us—the people right in front having to make some excuse, such as rearranging their jackets on the seats, to get a better peek without being obvious. It was sort of funny.

Despite the attention we got, we had a good time. MB was awake most of the time, and raved about how this was "the real thing; this is what it's about." He was all fired up that Billy Graham was here, and that there was such a crowd, and that so many people came forward at the end of the speaking. "He spoke the truth," MB declared. He limped down the street praising God.

MB doesn't fit normal "Christian" categories very well. He's amazing the way he trusts God, and doesn't complain about his situation or try to manipulate with his handicap. He doesn't seem to worry about anything. But I'm not so used to having one of "the least," with whom Christ identified himself, be alcoholic Muslim (Baptist!). It does work on your mind, and heart, walking slowly down a cold street at night with a crippled Muslim, who's about to spend the night outdoors, who is praising God for a Billy Graham crusade. That's the mark of a good teacher, I suppose.

He spent the night in my home. How could I just drop him off somewhere? For now, he's in a place—not great, but warm, furnished, meals; and soon to enter an alcoholic treatment program.


March 1995

Dear Friends and Relatives:

I have dreamed for some time of the possibility that some of my people in the community ministry would have the opportunity to go to other countries and be with people there who are also poor. I believe that such an exchange would stir *something* (I don't know what) in the heart of my people here.

Poor people are used to having people do *for* them when it comes to "charity." But much of our work here has been to find ways to work and be *with* people, as *partners* and as equals. For me, this falls under evangelism and empowerment, because most of the community seems to be "sheep without a shepherd." So, we continue in teaching and forming community that is an alternative community— namely, the Body of Christ—which operates by different rules than the street: respect, love, care, reliance on God. There is power in such community and there is dignity. We have just elected a new Steering Committee in the first co-op, and it is a joy to meet with these new members, and feel how seriously they take what we are doing, and experience their desire to work at making the co-op succeed.

In a TV documentary about Mother Teresa, she said the poverty in the United States is the worst she had seen in the world. That struck me as odd, because I know that there are shack towns, hovels, acres of destitute people in many of the undeveloped countries. So, I can only interpret Mother Teresa's judgment to mean that here, in what is arguably the wealthiest society in history, she sees people who have no dignity, who are beat down, who have no sense of community; people who are poor surrounded as nowhere else by a sea of wealth to which they have no access, and by a majority which despises them and fears them, and a majority which is, in large measure, of a different color.

Somehow my sense is that people in other countries, who may actually have less materially than even poor people in the U.S., have much more in terms of their sense of self-worth and community. And they may have less psychological and emotional pressure beating on them from the surrounding society.

My desire, as I said, then, is to have my people go be with poor people in other countries, to get these two types of poor people together. And now it is going to happen! An organization called PATH, Presbyterian Answer to Hunger, of which I am a board member, has offered to pay the expenses to send two people from our food co-op on a trip to Nicaragua in June. I get teary-eyed writing about it yet I clearly see the Lord's hand in this. I was not expecting this to happen—I have just joined the board, and I did not seek out the position. At our very first meeting, I voiced my hope of seeing poor people be able to communicate and minister to others, exercise their own gifts and talents and not just be ministered to. The director of PATH, Sarah Humphries, was immediately taken by the idea and began to work on it. I am very grateful to her, and am clear that this is something the Spirit has brought about.

So, June 16-25, two of our members will go with a group of other church folk to Nicaragua, to the area of Esteli, to visit a joint project of the Presbytery of Greater Atlanta and CEPAD (the Council of Evangelical Churches of Nicaragua). Our new co-op president has already said yes to the trip, and another person is praying about it.

Our co-op anniversary celebration was great. Dr. James Denison, pastor of the Second Ponce de Leon Baptist Church, spoke and was very encouraging to us about what we are doing. The "Mighty Genesis" singers raised the roof with their gospel music and our own cooks prepared a fine meal.

I continue to be grateful for you who help me to keep going here. It is absolutely the case that without your kind support, I could not continue. I thank you.


April 1995

Dear Friends and Relatives:

Two people have come forward for the trip to Nicaragua. We have to do what it takes to get everything ready now, though I am confident the Lord will aid us to work out the details regarding passports, etc.

Our community ministry work, as I often tell you, especially through the co-op, is about people taking responsibility for their own lives in the name of the Lord. There are, then, two sides to the coin: (1) people growing in their relationship to Christ; and (2) being empowered by the Lord in their work together to take responsibility for this co-op and for the possibility of still other structures which *they themselves* might create (e.g., the second co-op). [A note here about #1 above—people are not required to be Christians nor do we proselytize, so in the case of such a person we are talking about the personal growth that would be important to him/her.]

Clearly, given the political winds, we are moving in a right direction. There is much talk of funding cuts, funding cuts that will affect poor people, and talk about the church taking over care for poor people and people taking more responsibility for their lives. Poor people therefore need to find ways to work together and begin to prepare for what will be even more difficult times ahead. We continue to work to aid just such movement, so we are surprised to have run into an unexpected roadblock in our efforts.

Last year, as you know, two members of our original co-op were granted funding from the Self-Development of People Committee of the local Presbyterian, USA, presbytery to begin a second co-op. It was indicated at the time that the funding could be renewed. But when Fay and Jackie applied for funding this year, they were turned down! The letter notifying them said "you do not meet the guidelines," though the second co-op is the very same organization that met the guidelines last year, and the guidelines have not changed. Of course, this has Jackie and Fay upset—they're just getting started well, really, since it takes a while to build up a co-op, and it's too much money ($12,000) to turn around and find somewhere else. Now they feel jerked around by the people from whom they least expect it, people they counted on to be in their corner.

Not long ago, the two of them (Jackie and Fay) went to a luncheon of local and national self-development committee members, and they were asked to say a few words. A national committee member said enthusiastically, "We have to listen to these people!" and Fay and Jackie came back glowing about how wonderful people had been to them. (They had been a little afraid to go to this meeting of "officials.") All this, of course, boosted their confidence that the committee was behind them. So being rejected abruptly with no warning or effort to work with them came as quite a shock.

I do want to say that the Presbytery of Greater Atlanta has often been thoughtful and supportive of our work, so I do not want to come across as "badmouthing" it. The way this has been dealt with is an aberration in our experience and I am not without hope that the decision can be reviewed—and reversed. Pray with us toward that end.

I also want to thank the Lord for providing a car for Fay. She has needed one for a long time. The car is 12 years old but seems to be in pretty good shape. Members of our church were instrumental in obtaining this gift, and we thank them.

Lastly, please consider whether you know of others who might be interested in what we are doing, whether corporations, associations or individuals, and let me know. I would be glad to talk with them or send a mailing to them. We are doing quite well, but still do not cover all our cost—once again I am in a position of borrowing money to pay FICA costs on my own income that I have not been able to raise. (They are last in the pecking order as we pay the bills.) The Lord continues to make a way, and I know this debt, too, will somehow be covered, but I, we, need some more monies coming in on a regular basis, either in monthly pledges or small annual grants.

## May 1995

Dear Friends and Relatives:

We are getting the picture pieced together, and we are not going to get Self-Development money from the Presbytery for the second co-op. Of course this is a great disappointment, but I am praying that we will be able to continue that second co-op. I am very grateful that the Lord has taught me to rely on God and not to carry this myself as a great burden, which I could easily allow to drive me momentarily insane with frantic effort to keep this co-op going and these two good people from losing the little jobs it provides. But I will continue to make the efforts I can and trust God to give increase.

The new (old) car that was given to Fay is already down. Apparently, the transmission is dead—the car will not move. Boy, it gets old dealing with so few resources—tests my faith!

I went with Hawk to visit one of his daughters; he seems to feel she has gone off the deep end mentally. She told me a gang in her area thinks she "saw something" and they are out to get her, so she is afraid to go back to her home. She is staying with another of her sisters who is in the co-op. Driving into her apartment complex is like going into another world—guys wanting to know if we want drugs—they are bold—empty apartments, boarded up. We're definitely talking third world! It is no place to bring up children, but they are everywhere. This daughter is going to stay with her sister until the end of the month—there are three rooms for the 13 children and 4 adults. If she's not crazy she will be. I honestly don't know how these folks make it; it is amazing to me there is not more crime and rioting. Actually, there is so much more than gets reported, but it is poor people taking the pressures out on each other. I have to say, the sister who took her in is an example to me, as I am not up to taking in a family of seven for 3 weeks!

Scarce resources! Not enough of what's needed! With all the talk about need for changes in the welfare program, I find myself thinking that the greatest changes needed are in our hearts, because I don't think resources are scarce generally, deficit or not. Changes are needed because we have left those who are poor to their own devices, in communities (should I say "ghettos") of their own, and do not see them as brothers and sisters, but almost as enemies.

Arranging our lives so as to be safe and insulated from those we don't know may be expected of "the world," but for *Christians*, the Lord makes it clear we are to have aggressive love for the "least of these." Instead of love, I think we, like so many others, mostly have fear, and instead of trusting God, we mostly look out for ourselves, all the while largely hiding from ourselves that this is so. Christians need to be moving *toward* suffering people, not away from them. On the whole, we North American middle-class Christians are more like the Levite in the story Jesus told of the Good Samaritan: we see the injured man and pass by on the other side. We seem to want to stay away from our injured, demeaned brothers and sisters, unwilling to be neighbors actually touched by their lives. This makes it easy to make decisions "about" and "for" "them. We are as quick as anyone else to blame the least for their plight. "They" are a separate and unknown group onto which we project our fears and about whom we make judgments. So, we move to the suburbs; we build more churches further out, concerned to gain members with means rather than poor ones; we are most uncreative about our calling to be "salt" in our cities. We seem captured by the American Dream, as if it were equivalent to the Kingdom of God.

I'm not saying anyone needs to try to be a hero; nor does it work to waltz in and try to rescue or change those who are suffering and poor. But we could be more intentional about forming colonies of people who can support each other in our cities as we learn to be neighbors in places that have become inhuman. Doing so would tie the larger community together anew in a way that relief efforts and programs cannot.

I find that there can be a rich exchange between people of different cultures when we get to know each other and can treat each other like real people. I know I am grateful to be where I am; my neighbors have enriched my life. This week, all the members of the second co-op were asking about my wife, Barbara, because I had requested that they pray for her regarding some health problems. (She's been better since they prayed!) It was touching to have so many of them ask. One woman gave me $5: she said she had gotten paid that day and wanted me to get something special for my wife. Another walked to the store and bought a local remedy for her.

At the same meeting, one of our co-op members, Jimmie K, gave the devotional meditation. He talked about love. He said, "Where there is love, things are different." He spoke the truth.

June 1995

Dear Friends and Relatives:
Two of the women in the Community Ministry (both members of the food co-op) will soon be in Nicaragua. I

need to get them to the airport gate by 7:00 a.m. tomorrow (the 16th).

One of the women came on the bus to my house tonight wanting $20 of the $50 set aside for her as travel spending money. I've kidded these two as we've worked to get ready for this trip that I am always wary about what is coming next. What will they call and tell me they need that they don't have? What emergency has come up? And sure enough—even though we are on the eve of the flight, and I thought things were finally all set, I get this message on my answer service in that particular tone of voice: "Chad, call me as soon as you can." Lord, have mercy—what is this about?

When it comes to money, it's amazing. I told her two days ago that I had $50 spending money for her to take (I was advised that that should be sufficient) and that if she wanted any more than that, she needed to find a way to provide it for herself. I should have foreseen this—that opened the door for her to spend the $50 *before* she even leaves! But it's not for herself—"Can I get twenty of that $50 for food for the little boy here for when I'm gone?" That, of course, will leave her only $30 to take to Nicaragua. *Thirty dollars* on her person in a foreign country where she cannot speak the language! Seems the important thing is to get through *today*—tomorrow she will deal with the consequences—arriving there poor, which is, of course, what she is used to.

He's not her little boy; there are other adults in the house, I argue to myself. But she is taking money that is "her" money, money she would have on this long, far-away-from-home journey, and spending it beforehand, leaving little for herself. Would I do that? Should she? I don't know, but I said, "OK"—what could I say? She's loving the little boy and I'm irritated. Yet I would want to have peace of mind when I left knowing that the child had food. But can I let her go with less than $50? I don't think so. But I don't have $20 on me to give to her to replace it and the banks are closed. So she will travel with less. She didn't ask for more and wasn't complaining. The battle is in me, not her.

I read a disturbing report in the local Open Door community's newspaper "Hospitality" for May about a talk show host named Emiliano Limon in LA of KFI radio advocating putting the homeless to sleep: "If homeless people can't survive on their own, why shouldn't they be put to sleep?" This was last July 9. "Hospitality" reported that KFI had neither apologized nor made equal time for opposing views. Scary stuff! I know Jesus's view of "the least" was sure different. When "they" are not neighbors.... (See May letter.)

One of the young men who used to come to the church some years ago is in jail for murder. The poor guy has had one you-know-what-of-a-life so it's no surprise. I haven't been to see him yet; haven't wanted to go see him, to tell you the truth. I know I will, but I have no trust that there will be any value to visiting him and I don't know what to say; he doesn't seem to listen. I guess that's what I'll say, at least partly.

Since I wrote those lines, I went to visit him, but they couldn't locate him (I'll try to find his mama and see if he's there under another name). But as I was walking across the parking lot, I heard someone hollering from high up in the jail (a very imposing 10 or 12 story building) on the left wing, shouting out one of the little windows, I guess. It took me a minute, but I finally realized he was hollering at me! "Hey, Rev, I'll be out soon and back to Summerhill. Tell old man Webby I'll be out soon and on Georgia Avenue." I waved, signaling OK, but I never saw anyone and don't know who it was. I'll find out sooner or later. Something about that made me feel like I'm really gaining a place in the community!

And since I started this letter, I sent the women off. I did find more money for their trip: I couldn't let them go with so little. I've got to have peace of mind, too.


## August 1995

Dear Friends and Relatives:

It is Georgia summer with a vengeance as I begin this letter: 102 degrees yesterday, today supposed to be hotter. Yesterday it was 92 by 10:30 am. and 92 again at 10:30 p.m. Neither in our home nor in the space where we hold our co-op meetings do we have air conditioning, and this kind of persistent heat saps me.

I visited the young man in jail about whom I wrote in June. He's the one I tried to see before but didn't really want to go visit. He's charged with murder and aggravated assault. He's 17.

He's different than I ever knew him to be. He doesn't know what he faces—life sentence, the death penalty? He wonders, "How did my life get to be like this? How did it turn out this way?" Seventeen and wondering how it turned out this way!

His life was difficult from birth: mother abused and addicted, no father around. He grew up alone. He's a person who will inflict pain on himself and others until something happens to change his direction. That something has happened.

He says, "I wish I had listened to you and people in the church."

As we talk, he breaks down and cries, covering his face. I've never seen him cry. I cry with him—I feel the weight of it. I wish I could touch him, put an arm on his shoulder, but we are separated by steel and glass. Like the rich man divided from Abraham in Jesus's parable we are kept apart by a barrier that I cannot cross. Truthfully, I could not cross to him before, when he was running the streets—now he cannot cross to me. He can see the barrier now; before it was invisible. He and his family have been erecting this wall from birth, and now circumstances are such that the curtain is pulled back, and we can see what they have been constructing—a jail, isolation, a barrier that comes from trying to use others for his own ends.

Seventeen seems too young to have to grieve your life, and yet, sooner is best under the circumstances. He says it's hard to live with what he has done (I think he claims self-defense, but he hasn't wanted to discuss the details), and thinks that God is punishing him. "Can I be forgiven?" he asks. He's got time to reflect. He reads the scriptures, prays and goes to church meetings in the jail. Facing a judgment on your life tends to sober one up.

As I say, he is already a different person. He is beginning to be able to see. He is beginning to grieve and to think new thoughts. To me, his incarceration is God's mercy, though for him right now it does not appear merciful, partly because he still cannot fully grasp and understand the depths of his own inner chaos and evil. But it is mercy—he is being pulled from hell, though to him it looks and feels like entering it. The very depths of his evil have become the catalyst to his salvation. He has bottomed out, but instead of being dragged further into hell, he is, I pray and hope, emerging. Yes, he faces the possibility of a long isolation, but it is also an opportunity, forced on him by his decisions. He must begin anew, and with pain (labor pain?), grieve who he has been and how he has lived, but also, by grace, rejoice as he begins to recognize the wonderful love and goodness of God.

I see how we, Georgia Avenue Church, were needed in his life. What we have done is not lost. There are echoes for him of things that are real and good. Something about what we gave him, the moments of care, the words of scripture and/or direction helps to direct his reflection and his prayers now. Our efforts to be faithful and caring aid with the new life emerging.

Despite the barrier of iron and glass, this day we *have* actually touched—for the first time. It is also humbling for me once again to see God's embrace on the life of one on whom I had given up. God is good.[3]

I want to thank you again for the ways you enable me to continue here. You are very kind, and I am grateful to you.

---

[3] This young man has been in prison almost continuously since that 1995 letter and has been notified that he *may* be evaluated for parole in November 2019. Based on the continuous care of our church, most particularly through one couple that has been so faithful to him, he has become a different person, a quite mature and serious-minded follower of the Lord. It has been a long and hard but fruitful road.

September 1995

Dear Friends and Relatives:

I do not usually write personal reflections in this letter, but I turned 50 not long ago and find myself ruminating some. I'm grateful to have lived this long and thankful, too, that God has freed me from some of my pride to be more loving and human.

I've thought especially about a dream/daydream/vision type of experience that happened to me a few years ago. It was one of those door-opening events, and it still holds power for me for the years since.

Atlanta is very privileged to have a monastery nearby, in Conyers. It is a Benedictine Trappist monastery, begun by members of the house at Gethsemane (Kentucky)—Thomas Merton's monastery—just over 50 years ago. I've been going out there on some basis for close to 20 years, usually spending one workday a month. It most definitely helps to sustain me. I am so grateful for the place and its people.

The sanctuary is a beautiful Gothic building. Formed of large cast cement blocks, of course it is quiet, as is the whole place, for the most part, and that is an important part of the emphasis that the monks maintain—"come aside to retreat, be silent...."

On this occasion, I was sitting in the sanctuary, in the back, high up in the balcony. It was still and I was quietly meditating (I thought I was the only one in the space) when the silence was shattered by an air hammer or chisel which started blasting away inside the sanctuary with no warning. I couldn't see it, but it sounded like one of the tools used to break up the pavement to dig under the street. Inside that building the noise "filled the temple;" there was no silence! (It's funny sometime how irreverent the monks can be about getting their work done.)

For some reason, I didn't jump up in disgust or try to escape the noise. Rather it seemed as if that jackhammer with all its noise was in my heart. I had been becoming aware that I was not really such a loving person, that I actually was "hard of heart." Now I had come to this place to be in the presence of the Lord, and when I had gotten set and ready and quiet, it was as though Jesus was meeting me with violent heart surgery, showing me how hard my heart was that it required such a tool to gain entry. Yet he also showed me his own love, in that he was still working on me.

I knew that I was to sit there until the jackhammer stopped and the Lord was done, no matter how long it took. And I did; I don't know how long that was.

That was the "vision:" it was a sign to me about what the Lord was working out in my life. I don't know why the Lord waited so long; probably because I was not ready, and had not really desired to be free to love. Generally speaking, I hadn't even known I didn't know how to love. I was sure of myself as a "man of God," pastor, religious person, and probably afraid to let others get close to me as well.

I owe much to my wife Barbara, my children, my brothers and sisters in the church and many of you who have been some of my tutors and jackhammers. Thank you.

Sometimes things happen that act as a gauge, help me to see how far I've come. A couple of weeks ago, someone broke into our home while everyone was away, stole some things and generally made a lot of work for us. I am glad to say I was able to do something besides curse! I was even able to sincerely pray for that person, so I suppose the jackhammer made some difference!! I wish I could tell you that I loved enough that I was only concerned for his wellbeing as a person and before God, but the truth is I also had violent fantasies about what I would do to him if I caught him. So that is confession; nevertheless, for me there has been definite progress.

The books of Joel and Acts in the Bible say, "Your young men will see visions and your old men have dreams." I'm not sure whether the monastery event was a vision or a dream, but the older I get, the younger I feel, so I guess it doesn't matter. The important thing is, I'm not abandoned. I like it. I'm becoming human, learning to love, being given a new heart.

October 1995

Dear Friends and Relatives:

There is more suffering imposed on those who are poor. Sometimes it causes distortions, sometimes it transforms into greatness. Living here, I benefit from the powerful struggles with suffering which people endure.

Barry is homeless and is an alcoholic. He doesn't think his addiction is *that* bad, but he knows it's a problem. He came to the Bible study today. Hardly anyone actually comes to these studies when they say they will. But he had told me two weeks ago he would be here, and here he was. I like Barry. He's about 6'4", talkative, 38. He can quote scripture better than I.

In 1988, an acquaintance threw gasoline on him and lit it. He became a human torch, burned terribly on his arms and torso. It's hard to imagine what he went through. One hand is virtually useless to him as the muscles and ligaments were burned off, but he has recovered most of his movement otherwise.

A man with this much suffering has great potential to minister to others, and this community needs what he could offer in recovery. He needs a lot of healing, from the inside out, and asks your prayers that he will face up to his addictions.

When we had the Wednesday lunch today, there was a good gathering of folks. During the worship time, Huey said he wanted to say a few words. Huey has a great face, white hair against his dark, lined skin. He started talking and was so graceful; wonderful cadence began to roll from him: "Before you can go up, you got to go *down!* (he touches his knees), "You got to get down on these and pray. The *Lord* will lift you up, but you can't do it yo'sef." His hands were moving, pointing in an energetic animated way. "I'll tell *anybody* what the man Jesus done fo' me!" he said as he pulled a little pocket Bible out of his jacket. It was great. Huey's suffering has created an unknown Demosthenes.

At one point during the last co-op meeting, somebody told me Walter Lee was upstairs, sick. I found him lying on the bathroom floor with his head between the urinal and the commode, under the stall partition. He had diarrhea and it was all over the floor and him. It didn't take long to decide I had best call an ambulance, not knowing what all was wrong with him. With my back trouble, I couldn't move him around. I told him to lie still.

I went downstairs to use the phone and asked Mark to check on him. But Walter Lee hadn't stayed down: on the way back up Mark met me to say that as he got up there, Walter Lee was falling, and he hit his head, hard, on the tile floor.

I went back into the bathroom—nobody really wanted to go in there. He was lying on the floor, thick, dark blood spread out around his head. He was dazed. He only has one eye, and always has a cold, so Walter Lee is an unusual figure. I sat with him on the floor, talking and praying with him, his glass eye staring at me—he needed someone there.

As I sat there with Walter Lee, waiting, I could not help but be touched by this lowly person, lying there helpless and poor and silent, created by God but so "nobody," so alone. He is harmless, a real Lazarus-outside-the-gate figure in many ways, given care only by one or two other poor neighbors who have concern about him.

Some people's beauty is obscured to my self-concerned eyes by their deformities and whatever it is about them that threatens me and puts me off. I had to pass through a great barrier before I could really see Walter Lee that day and allow myself to be ministered to by him—the barrier of the fear of sickness, the barrier of the diarrhea and foulness, the barrier of his bloodiness and his strange appearance. I do not know what all allowed me to cross that barrier, but I thank God. It was worth it: being with Walter Lee was one more unexpected gift.

I know that I contribute something to this community, but it sure is not one-sided. The Lord gives me a lot through these unpretentious sufferers at the bottom of society.

November 1995

Dear Friends and Relatives:

This Thanksgiving I know that I am very blessed, and I am thankful to be where I am, with the people I am with, doing what I am doing. I sometimes have thought how great it would be to be a baseball player and be paid to play a game you love! But I am in that position in many respects—I love what I am doing and the Lord has made a way for me to do this work and be provided for at the same time. I am grateful to God at this Thanksgiving season. I am truly a rich man.

Many of you are instrumental in that. I cannot thank you enough.

It's November, so I ask you to consider any changes in financial support that you might need to make. Some of you have been so faithful for so long, and yet I know circumstances change. If you want to make any kind of change in your commitment to this work, please do not hesitate, even if that change includes stopping or lowering your contribution. It's not that we don't need help, and next year I will need to raise more than ever to keep the second co-op going, but I would not want anyone sending money to me that caused hardship.

Financially, we mostly make ends meet—but not quite. We have so far always fallen short, and when we do, I absorb the cost. Last year that was about $1800, for which I am still in debt, and this year we are behind about $2400 at this point, with prospects of some help before year-end. Pray for us that we might by the grace of God be able to end the year in the black—I would even dare to hope that we might erase the past debt. I will send out a year-end financial report sometime in the spring.

Last month the co-op members planned their own fundraiser to help provide for food costs, and it was very helpful. The gospel band, "J.T. Hatten and the Mighty Genesis," performed for us, and it was quite an event! We held it in the church sanctuary—loud! One couple got into a fight in a front pew, momentarily taking over the entertainment, but otherwise, things went quite well and the event raised $200 for co-op food. It was more than just the money that mattered—it was another act of people in the co-op taking responsibility to keep the co-op going.

With regard to the work itself, we continue to provide food, counsel, emergency assistance, an alternative place and teaching to the harshness of daily temptations, pressures and realities. We—meaning to some degree, you—bought and distributed approximately 43 tons of supplemental food during the course of the year for about 80 families of the co-ops, plus for many other folks who obtained emergency food. I continue to make hospital, jail and home visits. (One sad visit this month was with the treasurer of our first food co-op the day after her 19-year-old grandson was killed on the street.)

This year, for the first time, all the organizations in our building—the Georgia Avenue Church, Southwest Christian Fellowship and The Family Place daycare – sponsored or had some hand in hosting an open Thanksgiving Day service and meal.

It's good to see the interaction of all these groups—it's good to have the two churches co-operating, and good to have the mix of people, rich and poor, black and white, educated and illiterate, conservative and liberal, working together to cook and serve, not to mention breaking bread together. The co-op folks were partners in this—not just recipients. Many of them offered to cook and serve.

I neglected to tell you in last month's letter, but Walter Lee was treated and released that same night from the hospital. I felt that was premature, but ... hospitals are under pressure, too.

As I finish this, being the slow one that I can be, it has turned from Thanksgiving to Advent/Christmas. I pray that these "Holy Days" will be a rich time for you.


January 1996

Dear Friends and Relatives:
    In the most recent issue of *The Other Side* magazine, John Cole Vodicka wrote a short article about a Georgian, Maceo Snipes. I had not heard of Mr. Snipes—he was an African-American in Taylor County. He was born in 1909,

and at the age of 37 was lynched by four white men. He was lynched because he had voted the day before, the first African-American to do so in that county. A sign was posted on the African-American church in Rupert, Georgia, reading, "The first nigger to vote will never vote again." That was July 18, 1946. He was a World War II veteran.

Almost exactly one year before Mr. Snipes was murdered, I was born in a Texas where race matters were an ever-present reality. These racial issues have been a driving force in my life. I was not happy with the racial values of the culture of which I was a part. I'm thankful for what I believe to be God's grace, which allowed me to see things differently, though it's caused me some trouble.

I expect that to be minority black members of this society is to virtually never be unaware of race. Being white, I'm just as sure I'm not aware of it to the same degree, I do not have to be, but I live with it daily as a reality nevertheless. I grieve that that is so in the way that it is. One can't live in Grant Park without constant awareness of race, both in individual relationships and seeing the effects on the community of the long oppression of a minority people.

My first year at Andover Newton Theological School, in Boston, I lived in the North End of Boston, the "Little Italy" section, in a building which was owned by the American Baptist Boston City Society. At the seminary and Harvard and other places where I took classes and spent time it was an easy matter to make friends who were African American. They would visit me, etc., and we would walk down the streets going to and fro. I was ignorant enough of the city dynamics to not comprehend how anti-black the area was. The word got out that I was planning to move blacks in with me. One Saturday night when I was returning home late, a gang, apparently a sort of little Mafia group enforcing neighborhood mores, jumped me and beat me pretty badly. Fortunately, as I view it, enough people gathered quickly enough to keep them from killing me. I remember very little of the whole episode, being mostly unconscious, but it affected me greatly, giving me scars of all sorts, some of which I still bear.

Truthfully, I did not "deserve" the beating in the sense they thought I did: I was not planning to move anyone in and not trying to challenge the neighborhood. I was just ignorant and did not have good guidance from the directors of the program, and other folk who were in charge of the project of which I was a part. The "crime" for which I was tried and condemned was that I had black friends.

This month, as a nation, and as a church, we celebrated the birth of Dr. Martin Luther King, Jr. Dr. King was not perfect, but he was amazing. When I read his words and speeches, it is to me as though an Old Testament prophet has stepped right out of the pages. There is some kind of divine irony involved in the fact that his name was King, for while he was not President, he was a true leader of our country, exhorting us to be faithful to our calling as a nation and also as a church. He exercised a unique kind of leadership, and like a king of old, was first in battle. There are scriptures in Isaiah which Christians use to help us understand who Christ was that fit very well the ways Dr. King was perceived: "For he grew... like a root out of dry ground; he had no form or majesty that we should desire him. He was despised and rejected by others, a man of suffering and acquainted with infirmity, and as one from whom others hide their faces he was despised and we held him of no account." (Isa. 53:2-3, NRSV). Dr. King was despised from the perspective of the majority. And he became the primary focus for his people and all of us of bearing the sorrows of our long racial oppression.

Dr. King is gone, but the hope, the dream he had, remains. It is a great hope, the hope that one day we will honor each other *because* of our differences, and appreciate the beauty of all the varied ways God has created us, the vision that one day we will truly recognize and embrace each other as sisters and brothers. Bring it soon, Lord!


February 1996

Dear Friends and Relatives:
     You know, living here, I can become pretty callous. Right at the moment, I'm callous especially toward men who come wanting something (usually money) from me. I get tired of it—guys wanting hand-outs, guys who say they

will work for money, but when you put them to work want to do as little as possible as sloppily as possible for as much as they can get; guys who come to the house drunk, come late at night, who say, "I'm coming to church Sunday," but who never do, or talk about how quickly they are going to repay what they are "borrowing," but never do. Endless stories, some of them quite ingenious, about why they need this or that. People I've been trusting turn out to be back into drugs or something and once again I am enabling somebody's addictions. It's a game: "can I get something (again!) from this guy?"

I'm not good with this stuff, and my patience wears thin.

I know that right now I am not seeing these men as persons, and I am not being creative or caring in my responses: My immediate urge is to say "no" (or much worse!) but I battle with myself about that, knowing it to be an uncaring response. But the truth is, I *feel* uncaring and only see an intrusion when I don't want one.

I suspect some kind of battle is going on within me. What is the battle? If I had to guess, I'd say there's still some part of me learning to just "be here" (after 16 years!), as opposed to having great and dramatic things happen or wonderful changes take place. I keep thinking I am past such stuff, but at times like this, I see again an old pattern in me, which reappears. Some part of me wants (needs?) to be able to point to great changes in people's lives that come from my actions. (I hate to see and confess that to you...!) It is a self-centered part of me that sees others, in this case poor people, as means to an end to satisfy me. It's a form of addiction of my own, some "cause" orientation that needs to keep affirming my worth by being able to point to something, someone, I've shaped up. I'm a "fix people" junkie, and when they resist change of my prescription, I get tired, and tired of them. My "love" at these moments proves to be quite shallow.

I am just getting in touch with this anew as I write this letter. Writing has been hard, and once again I am late. When I start feeling tired or down, as I am, which relates to the callousness I spoke of earlier, I know something is going on. And often, at a spiritual level, it has to do with breaking those deep patterns of self-concern, fear, need, and pride.

I am grateful for the Lord's mercy and patience. Thankfully, Christ is actually much less judgmental than I toward me, and much wiser about what I truly need.

I've got a hunch that writing this letter—examining and confessing these things—may free me a little to move on, to answer the door to see a person, not a cause I need to fix, and just generally "be here" and be a neighbor a little longer. Thank you for listening.


March 1996

Dear Friends and Relatives:

The fifth anniversary celebration for the food co-op was really fine. Annie Kelley cooked a magnificent meal for the head table—she always insists on doing this, so whether we are planning to really have a head table or not, we are going to have a head table and she is going to prepare food for it: great collard greens, sweet potato pie, meat loaf, potato salad, tossed salad, corn bread, and macaroni and cheese. Then there was ham and of course, my black beans and rice—all topped off with brownies and ice cream. We did not lack for food! You missed it, and our evening was less joyful because you weren't there, but we managed to swallow our grief and have a good time anyway.

And the band—my, oh, my, what a show they put on. But everybody kept their clothes on and we didn't have to throw anybody out. No fights. All in all a great evening and we probably broke somewhere close to even.

Atlanta is one of the cities that was awarded an "Empowerment Zone" grant of $100 million from the federal government to be given out over a ten-year period. Twenty-nine zones, which have a high unemployment rate and many social problems, were identified to be recipients of the money. Supposedly the money is to go to grassroots folks to create jobs and enhance the wellbeing of the residents of the zones. The area in which I live and serve includes two of those zones—Grant Park and Summerhill. We haven't asked them for money as I have had the understanding that since we do religious teaching, we cannot receive federal money without compromising what we are about. (I am being given to understand that that in and of itself would not keep us from being eligible, so we will pursue this as a possibility for funding.) However, we have been told that our food co-op is getting a good bit of notice at the Empowerment Zone office, and some of the staff members came to see what we are doing. They are apparently planning to put food co-ops in all the zones, and yet ours is the only co-op of poor people of which they are aware. All of that is interesting, and makes me wonder what all God has been preparing that the future will reveal.[4]

We have once again been given money by the Presbyterian Answer to Hunger (PATH) program to send two people to Nicaragua. We have in the co-op a family that has eleven children. The father is crippled from an on-the-job accident and cannot hold a regular job—his hip is messed up badly. I like his spirit and he so wants to make the trip. The people in Nicaragua have encouraged him to come on. The wife's mother said she'd be glad to keep the children. The co-op Steering Committee has given the two of them its blessing, so they will be travelling abroad!

When would these two ever get to another country? When would they have the chance to take such a trip? I'm excited about a couple going. We do have a budding relationship with the Nicaraguans, as we sent two people last year, the food co-op folks sent money to support a child there and sent a box of school supplies to them. I'm believing this is a plant that is going to grow. I and we are very grateful to the PATH folks.

Percy, another member, had let me know he really wanted to go. But Percy's drinking is a problem from which he cannot get free. I owed it to him to be honest with him— I told him we had chosen someone else, and the reason I didn't back him was because of his drinking. He said, "My drinking is costing me a lot." Having the co-op and what it

---

[4] Nothing much came of that Empowerment Zone program and, in fact, it turned out to be one more large money boondoggle with everyone wanting to know "where did the money go?" A few folks, as I recall, were sent to prison.

has to offer and the relationships it brings makes that cost evident and makes people think.

I am conducting a baptism class right now that has four students in it, all girls. One of them attends a Catholic church, but decided to join her friends at the class. She told me she gets things on her mind and worries, for instance, about the gangs at school and the ways they threaten her and others. She is 12 years old and has a stomach ulcer. It's a tough scene for our kids here with the poverty, violence and stress. Come, Lord Jesus.


April, May 1996


Dear Friends and Relatives:

The Olympics are upon us here, and the organizers and builders are under the gun at this point. I live pretty close to the new stadium, and the Olympics are set to begin on July 19, my birthday. (By the way, last year was great, as Barbara surprised me totally on my 50th with a marching band that came down the street to our house, but this party will far surpass last year's.)

I have mixed emotions about the Olympics. It is a wonderful event with many ideals attached to it and a long and glorious history. It brings with it starry-eyed dreams and the discipline of young people, many of whom have sacrificed much and who wish to prove their skills and overcome obstacles and opponents before a worldwide audience. There is nothing else to match it.

On the other hand, it was touted and pushed in Atlanta as a huge economic boost. There is big money involved. When economics become the big thing, with a large dose of idealism and the image of our fair city thrown in (we want to look good "for the world") as justification for doing whatever, then you-know-who starts being pushed around—poor people. Who wants a stadium built nearby? *Nobody.* So, where we gonna build it? In the neighborhoods of the ones who have least power to say "*No!*" One group of such folk lives near me.

So, some of my people have a stadium being built in their backyard, with the accompanying sewer and water systems, etc. Blocks of homes are disrupted—streets blocked off, torn up. Huge machines are going day and night. Children who go to school cannot sleep, nor play outdoors. Water is shut off for days at a time, and when it is on, it runs red—there is too much clay in the water to use it to bathe, drink or cook. You can't use the bathroom in your own home. There is mud and debris all over the streets, and workmen urinating in empty lots in broad daylight because there aren't anywhere near enough porta-potties available. Jackie, one of the coordinators of the second co-op, has moved out of her home because it is unlivable. Most can't do even that.

Those who have the power and clout to make the decisions do not want the stadium problems, traffic and parking in their neighborhood. "But think how wonderful the Olympics will be for *Atlanta* (even if not for *some* of Atlanta). Some people just have to pay the price for such a once-in-a-lifetime thing"—and those people just happen to be the ones least able to pay it and least able to refuse it. Somebody's picture of what will make *Atlanta* look *great* and bring huge economic benefit to the city is being carried out, but it is not everybody's picture.

Nor will these poor be seeing any Olympic events. They can't afford the tickets. Nevertheless, they are paying a high price for the games. They, too, are sacrificing (and being sacrificed).

Meanwhile, much housing is being bulldozed to beautify the area. Occupants are given some money to relocate, but there are fewer and fewer places to be found. Add to this landlords who are kicking out their tenants for prospects of reaping big money during those two or three weeks...! It's funny how different something like the Olympics can look depending on your perspective.

I wish that the Olympic spirit could truly include us all, even our neighbors in our own city, not just our neighbors from around the world. Then the Olympics would be something glorious.

June, July 1996

Dear Friends and Relatives:

Already our co-op traveler has returned from Nicaragua. Kenny Redding could not say enough about how wonderful the people he accompanied were, nor about how gracious the Nicaraguans were. It was a revelation to him to have homeless children grabbing hold of him in Managua, begging for whatever he would give them. (Estimates are that *6000 homeless children* live on that city's streets!) Kenny's not used to being perceived as the rich one!

Kenny worked on two tasks: he helped distribute eyeglasses and he worked on building a school building. ("They have no books, no pencils, no paper... nothing!") He's ready to go back. Other people I've talked to who went on the trip said Kenny was *great* to have along, and the Nicaraguans loved him. (They loved the fact that he has a large family, too—eleven children!) I do regret that his wife ended up unable to go.

Kenny began to have a shadow of concern come over him on Thursday. He felt something was wrong at home and he couldn't shake it off. He called on Friday morning to find that his brother had gone into the hospital and was not expected to live, so he came back a week early to be with him.

He asked me to accompany him to pray with his brother in the city hospital. He's thin; after the immediate crisis, the doctors have told him he has maybe 6 to 7 months to live. He was open to talking about it, so we talked about dying, about his dying, about the regrets of his life, about matters concerning which he needs to repent. He's stuck in bed with nothing to do but contemplate his life and death. He wanted to know how to pray. I find these conversations about matters of importance in life deeply satisfying. So many times these diseases, disasters, afflictions end up as turning points for us about the ways we approach life and God. I'm not one who believes that God afflicts us with cancers, AIDS, etc., but they sure have a way of sobering us up, and the potential to lead us to true health. These forces that are bigger than us push us to look for providential help, when otherwise we consider ourselves free, wise, independent and strong. It is a lie, since we are in fact fragile and weak, but it is a lie that backs up our view of ourselves as "in-charge" (at least of ourselves).

Really, it seemed to me beyond belief, he left the hospital, looking much better. But he died soon and quietly at home. I am grateful to have had a hand in helping to prepare him for that moment.

When we have our co-op meetings, we normally begin with prayer, and, most commonly, the one who leads this will ask everyone to join in the Lord's Prayer. This one woman in our co-op always misstates the prayer to say "...forgive us this day our daily bread...." Something about that always touches me, hearing this poor person leading all these other poor people to say "forgive us this day our daily bread," bread which is already hard to come by. On the other hand, I think it is a good misstatement for many of us.

In the parable Jesus told about Lazarus and the rich man, commonly referred to as "Dives" (for "rich man" in Latin), it has really come home to me lately how much they needed each other. The rich man had a certain kind of possession that the poor man needed for life; the poor man offered the rich man the opportunity to escape from his golden chains and to move toward Life. If the rich man had not created such a chasm or wall, they both could have had what they needed, in this life and the next. But as it stood, Dives could not see Lazarus as his brother, but only as someone lesser, untouchable, worthy only of contempt. What a shock it must have been to his hearers to have Jesus end the story with the rich man (obviously blessed of God with his wealth) in hades, while the filthy, poor, sinner Lazarus ended up in paradise, with Dives' fence having become a huge chasm still keeping them apart! Dives needed forgiveness for his daily bread, and unbeknownst to him, he needed Lazarus. I think that parable is a pretty fair approximation of our situation in the U.S. and much of the world today.

September 1996

Dear Friends and Relatives:

I am writing this at the church building (usually I write at my home). As I write, a group of folks from the co-op are downstairs cooking for the Wednesday lunch. It will be an adventure—the fourth Wednesday is always a large crowd, our folks are preparing the meal for the first time, and we have a little less food than we thought we would. It's all rather exciting! I'm sure I won't be through with this letter before the meal is served. I'll let you know how it comes out.

Two women came to my office on Thursday two weeks ago. Between them they have eight children, none of whom had started to school yet because they had no clothes or shoes to wear. School had started about ten days earlier. They have no electricity or gas on at the house. I called Fay who said she'd work at getting some things together. She began to call other people who are in the co-op and/or church. Between them they came up with a good many things for the six girls in the families.

I get perturbed at people who are so thoughtless about their children. They could have come to me a week *before* school with the same problem and we could have had those children ready to go to school. That is the deeper toll of poverty—too depressed to care, to act; beat down. I am sure they are both very tired, and alone, and there is no light at the end of the tunnel. I want for them to turn to the Lord and become part of a caring people.

When Fay got the clothes together and delivered them, one of the mothers had already moved somewhere else. She and her brood are urban nomads, hidden wanderers of the city, looking for a hospitable oasis, a place to stop for a little while. Then they will be moving on, and then on. Maybe they are not technically homeless, not on the street, but they have no place. For the one who stayed, it's just a matter of time; she, too, will soon be moving on, as she obviously has no money to pay her rent. I'm sure those children grow up with a completely different reality in their heads than I have in mine. I expect we could be from different planets.

Two of the co-op members called today, two women again. Their husbands were both recently jailed and they wanted to make sure they could still get food, as they would not have the $4.00 they need to catch up their co-op fees. Of course, they can work it off, but I said we would give them some time. Four dollars! If you reflect on it some, it does not take long to see that such poverty would affect you—change your outlook, your ways of thinking, ideas that you would consider unacceptable become possible!

Well, back to the meal—it was a *resounding success*! Rave reviews, and the cooks were so proud of themselves. Annie Kelley supervised and she's a Mean Mama in the kitchen! She got it done, too, with the help of her crew. We had plenty and I ate too much.

You know, I can't do that much myself. But as I look about, I see a little bit of a community forming with my co-op people and others who hang around the church building. It is an alternative community. It's a slow, growing process, but I do believe it is real. I can call Fay for help—I do not have to do it all myself; and the poor people in the co-op can get together some things for others, and they can cook for others who need food, and we can collect school supplies for Nicaraguan school children, and together we can make our co-op work, and we can pray for each other. Together they take on ownership and form ministries in this place and, like me, find themselves being reshaped by the mix.

What we have here is so far from perfect. But there is something here that is real and good, something the Lord is bringing to pass. It's nice to be part of it.

I would love to see us branch out in some ways, and I believe that may happen. It would be great to expand our food to regular produce and groceries, adding them to our Food Bank leftovers and Sevananda rice and beans. It would be a natural extension of what we already do.

Even this dream must wait on the Lord: "If the Lord doesn't build the house, the work of the laborers is in vain." There is too much here I *still* do not know—there are too many ways I am not a part of the *other* community of which my folks are a part. There are things hidden from me—who's selling booze at night and putting on a good show during the day, for instance. Little by little I learn things and little by little folks' hearts are convicted. The wheat and the tares are together, not just in my heart, but in this (and any) group of folks. We need to have a sense of who can be trusted, who is solid enough to take on more weight, more responsibility, and we need to know the gifts folks have. That takes time and observation; it's slow but more solid. It's like a plant growing, but as small as our plant is, there are some blossoms and there is some fruit. What great joy to be in this place!

October 1996

Dear Friends and Relatives:

Waddell died last week. It was a surprise to us. He had cancer but didn't tell us. We learned of it pretty late and only after he had quit coming to co-op meetings.

Waddell was 67. He was such a gentle soul with a great wide smile that covered his face. Quiet and helpful.

He had a girlfriend, it seems, to whom he was devoted. Unfortunately, she is addicted to drugs, and she would do whatever it took to make Waddell give her his social security money, even if it meant he went without food. Reports are that she threatened to shoot him, said she would beat his head in with a hammer, and who knows what all, to get her way. But he wouldn't leave her.

Waddell was in co-op #2, the one that Jackie and Fay began. They found out that he had cancer, and Jackie spent about four hours with him at Grady Hospital that Tuesday. Sometimes Jackie gets overwhelmed with the demands of the co-op, getting the food all sorted out and everything and everybody taken care of. Meetings can be harried. Waddell told her, "You gonna be all right, Jackie. You gonna be all right." Something about that dying man's parting words to her meant a lot.

And she ministered to him. He wanted some watermelon. Jackie said she didn't have any money on her, but she went and got the chaplain, who was able to get what was needed. And then she asked the chaplain to visit, which he did, and Waddell said he wanted to be baptized before he died, which the chaplain also did. He was at peace.

Waddell died Thursday. He and Jackie had ministered to each other.

This is such a blessing to me to see Jackie and Fay minister to their people. I had too much on my plate to be there with Waddell, but Jackie could. Clearly, from the way she told me about it, she was grateful to have been there, and she knows her presence made a difference to this dear little man.

Jackie is becoming a different person than she was before the co-op, and she knows it. She says, "I'm doing better. I'm a lot more patient than I used to be." And that's the truth—she really works hard to keep her temper under control and care for the people in her co-op (a far cry from the woman who used to be so ready for a fight. By the way, I asked her permission to write about her.)

Last week, too, we witnessed in Atlanta the gruesome murder of a five-year-old boy, and the subsequent abduction of the mother and others in the family by a jealous boyfriend. One block from my home this man cut the little boy's throat after stabbing him. The woman's screams drew me from the house, but there were many police who would not let anyone near. I did not know them—seldom did I see activity around the house, but the mother was the niece of one of our co-op members. Thankfully the assailant let the others go and finally gave himself up.

We need to be here. There is such craziness and evil. Not that I am the savior of anything—I'm not, but people who are followers of the Lord need to be part of the mix and not make a point of running from scary situations. Of course, these things are disturbing to my children (we didn't tell them all the details, but they heard the screaming, too), but I know I am where I am supposed to be, so I also believe and pray that God will somehow use these things for their benefit. Barbara's a great mother to them, talks with them well about these kinds of issues—better than I—and invests a lot in them as a homeschool teacher. I am grateful for her and for her certainty also that we are in the right place. If we were not together in this we could not be here.

Speaking of my children, they are my sometimes helpers at getting this letter in the mail, especially when I am running late (as I most often am). If you don't get an envelope or something else is wrong, it may be that I did not give my workers good instructions, or that they got distracted by most anything. Add to their snafus how terrible I can be with details, and the possibilities of something going wrong are pretty strong. So, forgive me if I mess up some way, and let me know if there is anything I need to straighten out.

Evil is great, but by faith I am convinced that in the great scheme of things, it is no stronger than a sandcastle built next to the ocean of God's goodness and love. That faith helps carry me through, and then when I see my people, like Jackie, who were unconnected, begin to have their giftedness blossom and minister to others, it is evidence for my faith. Thank you so much for your part in helping me to be in this place.

November 1996

Dear Friends and Relatives:

For me, November is always a time of summing up and giving thanks. I have much for which to be thankful.

I am first of all thankful that we continue to continue. The Lord has kept us going and we have continued to grow as well. Since last Thanksgiving, we have distributed nearly as much as last year (83,000 pounds of food), despite the fact that we did not get the free USDA food to go with it for most of this year. And we now have 91 co-op families, thirteen more member families in our co-ops than we had last year at this time. My good partner, Mark, continues to be blessed with the patience to endure me and much other stuff that tests one. We have continued to get good foods, Sevananda has continued to supply rice and beans at a price we can afford, Fay and Jackie continue to work well together and do good work for their co-op. I am in partnership with wonderful brothers and sisters, and grow in my sense of community here in this place. And I have a lot to learn, so I have much to which I can look forward. I have a wonderful family and a warm home with the food I need.

I have not done as well financially this year as I have in some, but I have not suffered, due to the generosity of one person who made a large gift that has carried us through and allowed me to continue to draw a salary. Each year is different and the Lord persists in seeing us through. Just knowing that it is the Lord's hand that continues to provide (you know it is grace when you are dependent on the gifts of others) is a wonderful feeling, though not something to be taken for granted. I pray that I will listen to God's direction for me and, inasmuch as I have influence over the directions of the community ministry, that influence will flow from a desire to see "thy kingdom come, thy will be done, on earth as it is in heaven."

I cannot be thankful without being thankful for and to you—you who read this and support me and this work in whatever way you do. Some of you have contributed a great deal to this ministry, and we are deeply grateful.

And my little church, Georgia Avenue—such good people who desire to do the will of God, and do it without fanfare and religious game playing—what a blessing! At moments, I am torn between my work in the church and my ministry with those who are at the bottom of our society economically, but I cannot let either side go. Both are so fine. I have enjoyed our church services more and more as they increasingly resemble a party. They are full of joy, though we share some awfully tough things at times. One of our members recently lost her job and the employer had no money to pay her severance or cover her last paycheck. Our little church easily came up with over $1000 above our normal giving to see her through the month (we are talking about 40 folks, with children—not many families and no one wealthy). She is already getting back on her feet; out of this her faith has grown tremendously and the joy we have as a group is that much greater. [I never have to preach sermons on giving or enter into denominational stewardship programs in order to get people to give; they start out generously and go from there (I'm bragging now!).] My goodness, for what more could one ask?!

But there is more for which I could ask, and I do. I am so grateful to have so much, but I am so pained to see so many with so little. There's the lack all around—people with lack of love, lack of loving, lack of ability, lack of necessities, lack of respect to them or for themselves or others, lack of rich relationships, lack of faith. Clearly more is needed. I can and do throw my weight into making sure my brothers and sisters have what they need, which in and of itself is good work to which to be able to apply my mind and hand, but I wish such work were not necessary.

Thus, we move from Thanksgiving to the hope and yearning of Advent. Come, Lord Jesus, come quickly: bring to us a new earth and heaven full of justice and shalom....

## December 1996

Dear Friends and Relatives:

Another year comes to an end, though following the church calendar, the New Year has just begun with Advent. It seems to me that Christmas tree we just brought in is so familiar—did we ever take it down?! Has it been that recent since last Christmas?

Once again, we have had the Christmas party that our friends at Second Ponce de Leon Baptist manage to pull off every year. They always do a good job and provide toys for many of our children.

We always begin the time together with a short worship service in the sanctuary. It has become a regular feature of that service for one of the women who comes to our Wednesday noon meals to sing a solo. She has come to this gathering for twenty years now. For the past few years, it seems she has gotten there late or she has had a cold or something, so that her singing has not been evident. She rushed in a little late this time, too, but she wanted to sing. The woman who was directing the service called her to come up.

The singer has gotten older, and her poverty has taken a toll on her. Recently she had borrowed two dollars from me (for bus fare, I think it was). I do not expect to hear about money again when I give/loan it [folks "borrow" from me (most can't really repay but to say "borrow" helps to cover their pride)—yet rarely even mention it again], but this time she came back to me about a month later, and said

"I was planning to bring your two dollars today, but I was so low on food, I had to have something for the kids, and I do not have the money." She had tears in her eyes—how could I say anything but thank you for mentioning it, and please forget the two dollars.

So, you see what I mean when I say poverty; and on whom would it not take a toll? Extra wrinkles from the worries about whether she can pay for rent or food; extra weight from not eating right and needing perhaps to comfort herself somehow and quiet those anxieties; no teeth at all, though she can't be much over 40—all these make her look older than her years.

But she stood up there and she was beaming, and my gosh, I had forgotten what a beautiful voice she has. It has been so long since I heard her in good form; I was not prepared for the incredible strains that came forth. She sang "We Three Kings," and then, by request, "O Holy Night." If you know that last one, you know there are some high tones involved. Having no teeth, she could not say some of the words right, but the notes just soared and effortlessly, it seemed, she reached great heights.

It made me cry to sit there and watch her sing, hearing that wonderful voice. Once again the hand of poverty's cruelty was clearly evident: had she been in the right setting ... had she had the right training...!

But she was not fretting her misfortunes or railing at God for the unfairness of it all—she was standing up there beaming, her wispy blond hair giving her a kind of pop culture-angel appearance. She was praising God—a "'voice' crying in the wilderness" of our inequities and the desert of poverty of all those poor faces sitting there watching her sing. Those kinds of moments get to me, seeing this poor woman, knowing what might have been—I really turn to mush. And I say, "Come, Lord Jesus, come quickly."

But the Lord may not be coming too quickly; who knows? And in the meantime, it is good for me to be here where I am. If I were not here, it would be easy for me to forget (no, more than "easy to forget"—I can move from here *in order* to forget) that those who are poor are people; they are my brothers and sisters; they have gifts and abilities, and they feel pain as I do. As it is, I want to seal myself off from the realities of these folks' lives and the truth that they are just like me except they were born into situations that severely limit their options in our middle-class society. I do not want to be really touched by the hand of suffering that daily strikes them.

But, of course, Christmas is about One who had everything yet gave it up to come and live with us, and took on all that the hand of suffering would deal. It's incredible to have a Lord who is such a brother! It is beyond me... way beyond me.

Blessings on you during this season.

## February 1997

Dear Friends and Relatives:

There is one correction I forgot to make to the article I sent to you last month. The article stated that members receive about twenty pounds of food at each meeting: members actually receive 20 to 60 pounds, depending on family size.

Our sixth anniversary was February 28. We will celebrate this anniversary this Saturday, March 8, beginning at 3:00 in the afternoon. We would love to have you join us for food, music, guest speaker and a talent show. If you can come, just let me know ahead if you can, but if you can't because this letter's too late, come on anyway.

Recently a gentleman who is in the produce business offered to sell to our food cooperatives at cost. This is a tremendous offer, though it is one that we will have to figure out how to take advantage of. The savings could be great for our people: at today's prices we could buy 50 pounds of carrots for $7.00! Fourteen cents a pound! Many of our people do not buy many fruits and vegetables because they cannot afford them; this offer makes them affordable. Jackie and I went out to visit with our newfound friend at the State Farmers' Market, and sure enough, he's got all kinds of stuff. More later on this.

I am "**online**"! I have done it! Actually, I've done it twice (!!) starting out with America Online, which I've already left. My address is **whale@avana.net** and I would love to hear from you. I trashed my former address book without thinking when I got rid of the AOL material, so I don't have any addresses right now. I suppose I can email this letter, too, to anyone interested (but I haven't got that figured out yet). Let me know if you're interested. I suppose it would save me a stamp, too.

One of our homeless men considers himself a songwriter. This last Wednesday he wanted to sing for us during the devotional service that Fay leads before the meal. His song was entitled "I'm Sending up My Temple." Fay gave him the time—he stayed seated, began to clap, closed his eyes, started tapping his foot and singing. He's not too bad, really; very expressive. At the time, I didn't understand all the words, but he told me later that it was about building a home in "another land," sending up the "construction materials" daily. The song seemed to be his version of "I got a robe, you got a robe...": "I got a home, you got a home, all God's chi'ren got a home." Later, he gave me the words and permission to include them here.

*There is a dream that I have dreamed*
*Of my heavenly Father home*
*And I'll be going there one day*

*Before I lay down at night, I raise my head toward heaven*
*I just don't know, just how soon...*

*Every morning, night or noon*
*I just don't know, just how soon...*

*I'll be sending up my temple...every day*
*And I'll be sending up my temple...every day*
(printed just as he gave it)

The song's simple—a prayer and cry—dreaming of having a home, a place. I don't know how old this man is— he doesn't look that old to me—maybe early 40s. But I know, too, to take seriously that he doesn't know "just how soon." Life expectancy is not that great here. He could go to that new home any time as precarious as life is for him.

He seems to think he's got a place here at Georgia

Avenue. I guess he does, for it seems to be that he has made a place for himself in my heart. I do know that I benefit from the faith of people who are not counted for much in our society, and such dreams, such cries to God, join me to folks like him, and help me to remember what is important and what I am to be about.

There is another fellow who's made his "home" down in one of the window wells of the church basement. He's got cardboards, a sleeping bag and other blankets and a sheet of plastic to keep them dry. We had some ferocious rains here last week, and his things got wet. I took him to the laundromat, and we dried his sleeping bag and a blanket.

This man doesn't want our help and he doesn't like shelters because he says they are nothing but trouble: someone's always taking your things, or some kind of fuss is breaking out, and he doesn't want the hassle. He'll only go to them when it is going to be severely cold. Keith has some kind of mild mental problems and he also is addicted to alcohol, though it is not often that I see him drunk. He's been living for some years this way, though only in the last few months in the shadow of our building. We provide him with help that enables him to get by, but still, it's rather disconcerting. I must honestly say I'm not prepared to take him into my home and give him a home that way, though again, I say, he is not asking me to, nor is he asking me to be worried about him one way or another. He acts as though he were quite content. He comes to church on Sunday, and often is dressed rather well—I don't know where he keeps his things. But he claims to be a member of the church across the street.

March 1997

Dear Friends and Relatives:

I have gotten so far behind; I never mailed my February newsletter to most of you. So, here it is for those of you who didn't get it.

For those of you who did get that letter, you are

being let off with light reading this month.

The March 20 *Atlanta Constitution and Journal* had an article on our food co-ops on the front page of the "city life" section. The article was pretty good (though I am now "Chet" Hale, according to the beginning of the account); I don't think it will damage us and may even do some good. It may be useful with regard to fundraising with foundations. I might be able to reproduce the article for this newsletter at some point.

Our model for working does seem to be gaining some notice and interest. The Atlanta Community Food Bank is planning a seminar, based on our experience, for folks who want to begin co-ops and have asked Mark and me to speak. All this notice stuff is in the Lord's hands—I am not interested in tooting our horn, for we have much yet to learn. Public notice scares me in one way, for when you are noticed more, you become a target more. But, as I say, that is in the Lord's hands....

I do thank you for your continuing support and trust of me and my work. I hope I am being basically faithful. I do so much thank the Lord, especially at this season of Easter. In Jesus, we have an amazing, amazing brother. I would that everyone knew that.


April 1997

Dear Friends and Relatives:

We have a new family in our church. The father has spent 26 years in prison, the mother has an admittedly colorful history. They have moved to Atlanta, and they have come to know the Lord and to live in new ways. He is much older than she, and they have a newborn son. They are really so cute: he is a doting father, loves to hold his little boy, and she's a devoted mother. They wanted the child to be dedicated to the Lord, which we did, of course, in the church. Moments like that are so joyful—I had the privilege of holding this baby, praying with and for them, doing my part to draw them into this family called Georgia Avenue Church, and having the experience of seeing them warmly embraced.

It's difficult for them. He has a form of cancer, which can recur, and in fact, since the dedication, it has recurred, which was a shock. We have laid hands on him and prayed, and are asking that this cancer be taken from him. They are on SSI disability because of the cancer, which means they don't have much income. They live in a public housing complex.

He started out as a teen-age gunman when it wasn't common, as it is now. He's been in shoot-outs with the police, "done it all." You wouldn't suspect all this if you met him—he's quiet, has a kind of scholarly air, likes to play chess and is good at it. Now he's doing something totally different from the old ways—and loving it.

We were talking together on April 16, and she mentioned having "lost some money" that day, and I asked the details. She had gotten a very late W-2 form from 1993 that had been sent to her mother's home. Why so late, she didn't know, but apparently, they had had difficulty finding her. She took this added income information to a tax preparing company that told her she would get "between 400 and 500 dollars back." But they wanted $120 to file for her, which she couldn't pay.

So, she went to the IRS office here in Atlanta in March. The person she talked to said it was too close to April 15; they would not do back taxes until after the 15th, as they were doing only 1996 tax returns until then. She came back to the IRS office on the 16th, to be told that, since this tax info was for the year 1993, the statute of limitations had run out on April 14, and she could no longer file for the return! So, the couple was telling me, they had just "lost some money."

For my part, I couldn't believe this catch-22 story had to be the end of it, so I went with her the next day. Any time I deal with the IRS I feel like Don Quixote jousting with windmills, but if anything is bigger than the IRS, it's the Lord, so we prayed and headed down there. We got the same story—they were sorry, but it was too late, and it wasn't their fault, because after all she had had three years to file this (she had just gotten the W-2). I said we would like to appeal it. The man said, "OK, but you need to get the papers ready and send with the appeal, so take a number and be seated."

And we waited. And waited. After two hours, we were called. The agent was quite nice, he did the figures (took *maybe* 15 minutes!) and said she would get back $37.00! "But they said I would get back 400 to 500 dollars!" He showed us the tables, and he was correct. He filled out the forms and said that since it was their mistake, he would backdate them and send them in. We had been steered to a human being! Indeed, a miracle had occurred!

They didn't get four or five hundred dollars, yet we had solved a mystery, and had some peace about it. But it sure left me wondering about that tax preparing company, which wanted $120 up front—and for so little work! From a person they knew was poor! They had to know she wasn't going to get back all that money. They were trying to rip off one more "gullible" person—someone who is vulnerable because of her need, who will go ahead and pay out money to get a quick return, who does not live as concerned or confident about the world of statutes and legalities. I hear so many reports of rip-offs of poor people.

It helps to be part of a "family," and not just out there alone dealing with all the craziness. That's what it means to be the church, though most middle-class folks are so "American individualized" there is little need of a larger family: they can, and largely do, make it on their own. If you're poor, a good church is an ark in a never-ending rain.

In May, I'll be away most of the second half of the month, as my daughter, Leah, is graduating from college in PA (congratulations! *cum laude*, too) and in June I am going as one of the co-op members to Nicaragua for 9 days. That will be an experience for me—I've never been out of the country except for a brief excursion to Montreal. Please indulge me once again and let this letter suffice for May as well. I would appreciate your prayers.

(The couple of which I write has read and approved this letter.)

June 1997

Dear Friends and Relatives:

I am back from Nicaragua, and glad. I am not used to traveling, having never been out of the country but for that brief excursion to Montreal. But I'm also glad I went.

The trip was adventuresome from the outset, as we missed our connection in Houston. This meant that instead of spending Saturday getting oriented in Managua, we spent the night and day in airports in Mexico City, San Salvador and Guatemala City. When we reached Managua, a city of 800,000, ours was the last flight, so they were closing the airport: they turned out the lights without giving us our bags (literally turned out the lights), and since the guard was sporting a machine gun, we felt obliged to leave the dark premises. All but one of us got our bags on Monday morning.

There was no hot water, period—we bathed and shaved in cold water, which took some getting used to. I got sick early on; from about Tuesday, Montezuma's revenge had a grip on me, which of course, made the trip less enjoyable and much more tiring.

Now that I'm back, I find it a little difficult to describe the trip. For the most part, we were insulated from everyday people by our schedule, by concerns about crime, by our inability to speak the language. I'm sure, given time and the chance, I could get much more at ease and used to things, but in 7 days I could only be a tourist. Yet, we met some wonderful Christian brothers and sisters, working under difficult circumstances. We visited a school that had corrugated tin for the roof and parts of the walls, and no floor but the dirt; we saw blocks of slums right across from the government buildings; we saw buildings still standing in ruins from the 1972 earthquake that killed more than 10,000 and left 200,000 homeless—buildings that people are now using as dwellings.

We were perceived as rich Norte Americanos, and besieged by requests, from beggars to pastors hoping their particular need would be the *one* the Lord would lay on our hearts to fulfill. It seemed beyond understanding that we might not all be rich and that in our country, I, for instance, am a beggar also, continually seeking funds to keep going. And indeed, I was rich there. In Nicaragua we visited those who were poor, but we lived like queens and kings while we were there, as I ate better at the hostels than I eat at home—meat at every meal and several times fish from the Pacific. It is strange now to awaken in my bedroom and know that the room is larger than many people's homes.

I do return with much understanding that I did not have. It is easier to see in that setting of such poverty the exploitation of the environment and the people, especially women, by those who have the money and power. Secondhand information, pictures, etc., cannot convey what one needs to know; for me, at least, it helps to go there, be there, and touch people to know that these are brothers and sisters. It made me want to work to give more focus to the trips for the future and strengthen the support for CEPAD. CEPAD is the Spanish acronym for Evangelical Committee for Aid to the Victims, an organization of primarily protestant/evangelical churches and denominations that came together to respond to the earthquake and have continued to work together to address the needs of the society. Many from the U.S. and other countries have joined hands with them. CEPAD makes low interest loans to people, works through "peace commissions" to disarm military groups, promotes environmental and health projects such as "dry latrines" and does all this in the name of Christ in a responsible, respectful way.

Kenny Redding and I went from the Food Co-op, with most of our expenses paid by PATH, Presbyterian Answer to Hunger. I want to express our gratitude to PATH, and also to several of you who helped with the expenses of the trip. Neither of us would be able to go but for your generosity. We thank you.

I want to also give thanks that in the last couple of weeks we were notified by United Way that we were awarded a grant of $6000 for the purpose of purchasing a truck. Our work now is to find the right truck for that amount, get it insured, etc. Keep us in prayer on this, as we need a truck badly. We're on our last leg with the ones we've been hiring. If you have any thoughts about where to direct us, they would be most welcome.

July 1997

Dear Friends and Relatives:

I realized as I was about to mail my late June letter that I would be turning around to get the July letter out, and that made little sense to me, so I am putting both on one page this time.

Unfortunately, it's too often the case that folks related to me are in the news, and not for good reasons. I am sorry to say that just before leaving for Nicaragua, one of the women related to our community here became notorious. Harriet has been in the news a great deal because she was arrested for allegedly "selling" her relatives' children for sexual purposes so that she could obtain drugs. Her case has been in the media so much here that nearly everybody is familiar with it.

It is easy and natural to condemn Harriet. Certainly, her actions, if true, deserve condemnation.

The problem for me, of course, is that I know Harriet. I do not see Harriet as just an evil person out there preying on children. I see a person who is desperate, whose world is awful and in shambles, who has lost her mother to drugs and whose father, Hawk (about whom I have often written) is infirm and no longer really available. She is a person raised with evil who has not been able to escape it, and as things get worse for her, she is sucked into the vortex of the evil, but truthfully, her desire in the past has been to do what is right. But she's overwhelmed and alone and out of control.

I haven't been able to visit her in jail yet, but I want to soon. I don't want her to believe she is abandoned, which is largely the case now. It seems even the members of her family shun her at this point, and even though none are model citizens themselves, it is easy to throw stones at Harriet. *Everybody* looks better than Harriet at this moment.

Somebody needs to write a book about Hawk's family. This daughter, Harriet, has seven children herself. (They'd all been taken from her prior to these alleged incidents.) His family would be one hellacious study in the effects of evil and the breeding ground for evil that poverty can be. I have talked about this before, but of all the families that I relate to, Hawk's stands out. His family has gone from being at the top of the heap to being at the bottom of the barrel. The evil of drugs and money that made them envied and wealthy has now made them shunned, poor, confused and death-oriented. Hawk, who has sincerely turned to the Lord, now lives with the daily agony of seeing the evil and devastation his former ways have wrought. He longs to be able to change it, and suffers at seeing ever-greater depths of malevolence well up from a seemingly bottomless pit. It's awesome and awful to behold—especially considering how many grandchildren there are.

Of the children I know, two have died of AIDS, the four girls I'm most familiar with apart from Constance (who is a faithful member of our church) have a total of about twenty-five children, and all the kids (again, Constance excepted) have dealt and/or used drugs. Their mother died addicted; their father made a name for himself and for his kids by dealing drugs and being a kingpin because of drugs. So far, the children cannot seem to overcome this legacy, even though it steadily takes them toward death. They are doing what they were taught and what gave them such happy times when they were kids. I know I've written about this before, but each new episode astounds me. I think I would call my book about them *Born in Quicksand*.

The children know the words about alternatives; they talk about the Gospel; they talk about God in their lives; they know those concepts enough that they are inoculated against the Holy Spirit. Harriet talks about having been "saved," and I don't doubt her word, but...!

My prayer for Harriet is that the time she almost certainly will be given in jail (though I do not believe she has been convicted yet), plus the separation from her family that this shame creates, may make it possible for her to think some new thoughts, turn some new directions. Yesterday on NPR's "All Things Considered" I heard about a Christian program in the Bronx that sounded great. It is a choir for addicts—a choir creates community. I know that we need some *strong*, loving and life-giving community-forming programs focused on the newness that God can give—traditional evangelism that deals only with the individual who is immersed in a dismal community will not cut the mustard. The co-op is not specifically set up for addicts, though it points in the right direction by seeking to create an alternative community of faith and life. (We need other people to come join us, too!)

I covet your prayers. These things get me down sometime.


August 1997

Dear Friends and Relatives:

I am beginning this on the birthday of my son John Luther, our youngest. He is 10 today, already into double digits, though he was born only 5 or 6 years ago. Amazing! I don't know how it happened.

We have been having some troubles in our second co-op, and misunderstandings have grown up over a few months now. I'm not nearly so firsthand involved in that co-op, so I am not always right on top of what's going on. One of the leaders, Jackie, had been absent a great deal because she had been under financial strain, and had taken another job, so had been missing Steering Committee meetings. She also does the shopping for the co-op, and since the truck had become unreliable, the shoppers were often *quite late* returning with the food, so Jackie would return feeling great pressure and it would be translated as gruffness and tyrannical haste. I think she felt responsible, too, or thought that others felt she was responsible, for these continuing problems. People's feathers were getting ruffled, and since she was not getting to the Steering Committee meetings, these matters were not being resolved. Instead, they were piling up.

I tried several times to sit down with Jackie, and with both of the primary leaders, only to have the meetings canceled for one reason or another. I did finally manage to meet with her alone, and obtained her pledge that she would indeed be available for the next Steering Committee meeting.

I don't usually go to those meetings, but I knew I needed to be at this one. When we all got together for that meeting, there was tension in the air. She knew people weren't happy with her, and she also knew she was upset at some of them, because to her mind they weren't doing as much as she but blaming her.

I had to begin the meeting with my own confession. I had told Jackie that I would make sure the truck would be there on time to pick her up for the most recent meeting. I had not done it. I got myself tangled up in other things, and I forgot that I needed to collar our truck driver to insure he would meet the appointed hour. He did not get there on time, and Jackie and the co-op members suffered because of it.

The meeting was difficult. For all our talk about respecting one another, when conflicts actually do arise, we don't want to face them and don't know how to deal with them. Jackie wanted to say, "I'm sorry" and "let's get on to more important things." "Why do we have to drag this out and make a big deal of it?!" Well, it was a sort of "big deal" and people needed to be able to say their piece, and, as it turned out, she needed to say some things, too. Slowly but surely, we actually did get at most of the issues. On top of that, the Steering Committee members expressed their desire to take on new tasks so they would feel more meaningful in their roles, including the job of getting Jackie to the Food Bank on time. We did indeed get most matters straightened out, relationships were restored, and we ended that meeting in a whole different atmosphere.

Fay told me after I returned from vacation that the Steering Committee had had another meeting since that one, and it was great. Furthermore, the new transportation arrangements worked so that the truck was on time, and co-op members indeed began doing their new jobs. The members of the committee even decided to hold a "clearing the air" session on a regular basis.

There is great joy in all this for me. "Life Together" as anyone who's ever been in a family knows, is going to have its difficult moments. The task is to take that conflict and make it work for you. Part of the intent with the co-ops is to create a family in which conflicts can be channeled to become the fuel for individual growth and community building. When we work with the strife in such a way that it draws us together instead of tearing us apart, and we end up with joy instead of bitterness, it is such a blessing. Of course, such is not the norm for many of us, and our people experience the resulting transformation as the presence of Christ among us, the Holy Spirit at work. We ended the meeting with praise and thanksgiving to God. What a gift!

September 1997

Dear Friends and Relatives:

Three weeks ago now, I had a most wonderful surprise. I was working at my desk when I got a phone call from the Atlanta Braves organization saying that they wanted to recognize the Georgia Avenue Food Cooperative. The woman who called said they wanted to give us 160 tickets to the baseball game on September 14, and they wanted six of us to be on the field for a pre-game ceremony at which John Smoltz would present us with a check for "at least $10,000!" Of course, I was dumbfounded—I don't think I even sounded excited at first. I sort of wondered, "What's the catch?" And then I wondered what all I needed to do for them first—usually I need to write a bunch of stuff about the co-ops, etc., but she said, "We've already taken care of it." Pure grace! I didn't have to work for this in any way. I began to feel excited.

It was an invitation we couldn't refuse. A number of church and co-op members went to the game, six of us went onto the field, and Chipper Jones, who filled in for John Smoltz who was pitching that day and needed to be getting ready, gave us a check for $16,667.00. What a blessing—more than we expected!

What will we do with the money? We always have ongoing expenses, especially salaries to pay and food to buy. At first, we were thinking of applying it to our efforts to obtain a truck, and we may yet add it to the money given to us by United Way for that purpose. But we are also hopeful that my associate, Mark, might be able to make the leap from part time to full time next year, and it may be best to put it toward the monies needed to make that possible. Deciding what to do is a great "problem" to have, and we are grateful to the Lord for providing the money and to the

Atlanta Braves for their gift.

Then there was the head scratching question, "How did this come about?" (besides, of course, the hand of the Lord). It turns out that some people in the Braves organization also work with the Atlanta Community Food Bank, and had turned to them for suggestions about organizations to support. They had recommended us and one other organization, which, along with the Food Bank, were also recognized. I have such high respect for the Atlanta Community Food Bank; it is truly a fine and solid organization. It means a great deal to have them also hold us in high regard. We are thankful to them for their hand in this, but also for many ways they have aided us in the past.

Speaking of the Food Bank, it is becoming more common for them to call us when they need a connection with some of the people who are receiving their food, since they deal with organizations who distribute the food, not the actual recipients. Because they are well known, they have become an important agency for others to call when they want information about local responses to hunger. One of their staff members called us last week to say that Channel 11 had contacted them about having someone on a TV show about hunger to help promote the city-wide "hunger walk" that benefits the Food Bank and organizations that use it. They called to ask if Fay, one of our coordinators for co-op #2, would speak as someone who "is in the thick of things." Fay was willing, and I took her to the station for the taping. She was "on" for a few minutes with the others they interviewed. She did a great job and right there in front of her on the screen with her name was the label "Georgia Avenue Cooperative." I am proud of her and a little amazed at the public attention that has suddenly come our way.

Public accolades and attention are great and fun; but it is not my intention to toot our horn, as I often say, either in this letter or to the public. If we receive notice, that is up to the Lord. My primary concern is that we keep our priorities straight—that we "seek first the kingdom of God..." that we strive to be faithful to the work at hand, that we give thanks and celebrate what God is doing among us and for us, and with any attention we get, that the Lord be honored.

Besides, as I am always aware, we've still got so much to learn. I continue to look at the Georgia Avenue Community Ministry and its food cooperatives as a slow-growing plant that needs constant nurture. It has already borne much fruit in the lives of our people, many mouths have been fed, much good has been done, but my sense is that it is still a tender shoot. But no need to worry, for The Great Gardener is at work in this place!

December 1997

Dear Friends and Relatives:

Advent is a season of the year with which many of us were not raised, even churchgoers who were not raised in liturgical traditions. I was raised Southern Baptist, a *very* non-liturgical group, and knew nothing about following a "church year." But at Georgia Avenue Church, we have been working for several years now at learning the church year, mostly with good results.

Advent is the beginning of that church year, and it has been, admittedly, somewhat difficult for us. Advent is to Christmas what somewhat longer Lent is to Easter—a four-week time of preparation prior to Christmas. Of course, Christians believe the Messiah has already come, but still, we *wait* for his return. Clearly, we do not live in the fullness of the reign of God yet, and we are aware of the power of the dark within and around us.

At the same time, we believe Christ is present with us even now. So we live with the creed that Christ has come, Christ is present, Christ will come again—we have been saved, we are being saved, we will be fully saved. Still, culturally for us non-liturgical folk, it is work to learn to take Advent seriously and celebrate Christmas *after* Advent, especially with our economy pushing Christmas so heavily from about Halloween on.

My belief is that we best *prepare* for Christ's coming again by being aware of his presence here *now*. Matthew 25's parable of the Great Judgment is perhaps the sharpest focus of this approach—the setting is "end time judgment" and Christ is zeroing in: "if you did it unto one of the least of these (then), you did it unto me." I must confess to you, however, that I do not always have eyes for the now. It is not always convenient for me to see Christ here—now. In fact, Saturday a week ago, I saw Him, but almost didn't recognize Him.

I was once again in the throes of getting ready for Sunday, and did not have much going for me toward an Advent sermon. I had to spend part of the middle of the day at the church building preparing for a music procession at the beginning of the service, in which I was to sing and play the recorder. I was the last to leave, and walking home afterward, I encountered a man who has some mental problems and who is, from time to time, homeless. He was walking toward the church. "Chad—give me a Bible," he said abruptly.

How many times have I given this guy a Bible?! He asks me this just about every time I see him. I was not disposed to give him another Bible. But seeing him reminded me I had forgotten to put a bag of food outside the kitchen door for someone who was coming to get it—which meant that I did need to return to the church. To my chagrin, Joe was happy to accompany me.

We got there and we went into my office, where he spotted some old Bibles I had found in a box (but forgotten). I said, "OK, OK." My attitude wasn't the best. As I was escorting him out, and heading down to the kitchen to bag the food, he said, "I'm just going to duck into your bathroom."

Now, these were words I was not glad to hear. They may sound harmless enough to you, but I have had experiences of people going into the bathroom and parking for a *long* time. And, as I said, I wanted to get back to my sermon preparation.

I took a while bagging the food. He wasn't out. I waited. I finally said "Joe, how you doing?" "I'll be out soon." I waited. "Joe, I'm needing to go." I could see through the door the floor was all wet and tell he was standing in there. "I'm coming." I decided to check the mail, which normally takes a little while. He was still not out. I waited. I finally had had it—I went pushing in, saying, "Joe, come on, I've got to get going."

And there He was: there was Christ, sitting on the pot! How could I force Him to rush, when it was cold and for all I knew He had no place to use the bathroom? I sure don't want the Lord telling me in the judgment "I needed to use the bathroom and you wouldn't let me do my business!" I backed out, humbled, and settled down for more waiting.

And you know, the funny thing was, all that time He was giving me the Advent sermon I was so worried about (and a monthly letter!)—and I almost missed it! All that waiting (Advent waiting?) was needed to open my eyes. The Lord is good.

May we all be blessed with eyes to see the Lord during this season and in the coming New Year.


### January 1998

Dear Friends and Relatives:

Bobby is 32 and was born nearby, in Peoplestown, the youngest child. He has two brothers and three sisters. One sister has died of AIDS, one of the brothers is in jail, one of the other sisters has had her children taken from her for abuse, as one of the babies died from neglect. The sons of the deceased sister are 20 and 21; they are both in jail. One of the sisters was married to one of Hawk's sons (who has died of AIDS); her twelve-year-old son was shot in the head a few months back, but has recovered well.

When Bobby was ten, his mother was killed—a great loss for him. She kept her niece from being killed by the niece's boyfriend by jumping in front of his gunshot. The sister who later died of AIDS raised Bobby.

Consequently, Bobby was pretty much on his own. He did go to school, though, and he actually enjoyed learning. They were too poor to get him much in the way of clothes and shoes, but he found a way to overcome that: he began to deal with drugs when he was 15—hustling on weekends—to provide for himself and his sister. He has continued selling heroin and crack pretty much ever since, except when he was in jail. He was making $500 a day—at his best $10,000 a week. But he's also been in prison five times, has spent nearly 15 years in jail, the last time serving 27 months.

In 1994, Bobby began to hang around the church, especially showing up for the Wednesday lunch. Sometime in 1995, he started to show up now and then at my Bible study for men. In August, he began to attend regularly, always pretty quiet. Attendance was always small at the Bible study, and once in a while, he would be the only one, at least for part of the time. This gave us a chance to talk, and Bobby got to the place where he was confessing what his life was about. He became a member of the food co-op and from early on was very helpful, carrying boxes for people who couldn't lift them, unloading the truck, helping setup and clean up. Mark and I got to the place that we trusted Bobby and would leave him to watch things or give him the keys for this or that. We, and the place, seemed to grow on him; he responded to the respect and interest we had for him.

In October 1996, a young woman who works in the daycare center here came into the picture for him, and eventually they began to talk about marriage (a daycare begun by a woman in our church and run by Christians). He commenced to go to church with her, and also found that a desire to be free of the drug habit and dealing was growing in him.

My partner, Mark, drove him to a drug rehab program some miles north of here in October 1996 (also begun and run by people of God). Homesick, he was back in three days, but his old habits were too strong for him. The young woman had the wisdom to call off the engagement. Bobby was at the bottom again. Before long, he entered a different rehab program and stuck with it.

He has graduated, marriage plans are back on track, and Bobby has found a job, with an organization, FCS, which is Christian—a job he's been in six months with good evaluations. It's a joy to see him and see the way he looks. When I talk with him, he sounds good, and he is ready to give thanks to God. He goes to AA meetings faithfully, and to church with his fiancé on Sundays and Wednesday nights to a Bible study. They are planning to be married in April.

Escaping the drug culture and its hold, the long-time habits and relationships, is well-nigh impossible. It takes the grace of God and it takes neighbors to provide new relationships, new possibilities, new thoughts, strength and opportunities. It's been a blessing to see how we and others have been a set of tools in the Lord's hands to free this young man.

Your gifts continue to make a way for me to be one of those neighbors, to live and work here, to be part of the mix. I thank you.

(Bobby has read and approved this letter)

February 1998

Dear Friends and Relatives:

One of our church members is a small woman from South Africa. For many years she was a political exile from her country. When she first came to us at Georgia Avenue Church in 1982, she was not interested in the church so much as the possibility of obtaining a house through the church, as her neighbor had done. At the time, she hated white people.

Soon after she came to the church and I got acquainted with her, she returned to Africa, to Ghana, where her husband was a student. After she had been gone some time and she was out of mind, so to speak, her stepmother called our church to say that Spanga was very sick and destitute in Ghana; she could not afford the medical help she needed; her sight and even her life were in danger. As a first step, our small church responded by taking up an offering, which came to about $400. It turned out that the money was worth so much more in Ghana that it enabled her to get the treatment and medicines she needed. She improved and returned to the US.

Once again, she came to us, this time her viewpoint somewhat altered by her struggle and our willingness to reach out to her. But her situation was grim and she was alone. I knew things were rough for her, and I asked three other leaders from the church to accompany me to meet with her to look at what needed to be done. The four of us sat down with her in her father's home, and by the time she laid out the whole story, all of us had drooping shoulders. How she carried the burdens, I don't know, because when it was shifted to us, we four men were weighed down. (1) She needed to go into the hospital for eye surgery; (2) she had three children, one of whom was a newborn; (3) her father had not been paying the house note, and foreclosure was imminent, so she would soon have no place to live; (4) she had no income and (5) her father had already gone to New York. She was alone, she had no money, she had children, she was sick, she had no place to live. We all prayed, and by God's grace, we each took on a part of the burden.

Members of the church took her children to care for, enabling her to go to the hospital for the eye surgery. We also found her an apartment and rented it. Now Spanga owns the home she lives in here in Grant Park (built by Charis Community Housing, a Christian organization similar to Habitat for Humanity). Her health, while not perfect, is vastly improved and she hasn't lost her sight. She is working at a local daycare center. She and her family are members of the food co-op; in fact, Spanga wrote the proposal that was awarded the grant that started our second co-op. She has been drawn close to the Lord through all of this, and no longer hates white people, but considers all the church members, regardless of their race, to be her family.

Even now it's not easy for Spanga. Her income is low and she heads a single-parent household. Her husband has never chosen to take responsibility for his family. Last year in the church, my wife, Barbara, and I were in the same small group with Spanga. Out of Spanga's sharing about her fatigue and loneliness, Barbara initiated a drive to raise the money to bring Spanga's mother from South Africa, and on Spanga's birthday, we surprised her during a church service by announcing that we had the money to fly her mother here.

Her mother, "Sis B," spent six months in Atlanta with us, ending last September. It was wonderful; Sis B is a dear, such a blessing to have here, not only with Spanga and her children, but with all of us. We didn't want to let her return home.

Sis B told us that all of her neighbors were afraid for her to come here. They were sure there was some trick involved and believed that there must be some evil that we white people had in mind. She told us that when she got back home, they came flocking to hear her tell about her visit, and make sure she was OK, and they would not believe how kindly we embraced her. In a way, it seemed as if Sis B could not believe it herself. For a black South African, this was a new experience. It was wonderful and terrible to touch the depths of pain that is the legacy of those apartheid years.

Her mother's visit has kindled a strong desire in Spanga to take her children, who have never been to South Africa, and visit her home country that she has not seen now for nearly 20 years. Most of the money has been provided, but she is still about $1500 short of the approximately $6000 needed. She hopes to make the trip in the summer. I am letting you know that Spanga has this desire/need. Some of you may be moved to help her make such a trip. If so, please send a check made out to Georgia Avenue Church, but designate it for "Spanga." Any money sent would go 100% toward making her trip possible.

These journeys of faith enrich my life. I love it, and I sure am glad to be here.


March 1998


Dear Friends and Relatives:

Thank you for your response to my letter about Spanga last month. $655 was sent to help her make the trip. I will keep you posted. I hope you do not mind my bringing that need to your attention. I will not make a habit of mentioning other situations for which money is needed. As always, I ask freely, leaving responses in your hands and with the Lord. I am grateful for your response, but there is *no* expectation on my part that you ought to respond.

I find when I talk to people who receive this letter that it is common for someone to say, "Well, exactly how does the co-op work?" It may be that one really needs to be here and watch what we do to understand, but I'll try to offer an explanation. For those of you who know all about this, you can skip the rest.

We have two co-ops, #1 and #2. #1 began February 28, 1991, after reading about such a model and discussing it with people who attend our Wednesday noon meal. #2 was kicked off September 9, 1994, with the leadership of Jackie Palmer and Fay Romero who had been members of #1.

Each co-op meets every other week and they both meet on Thursday, so every Thursday morning at the church one or the other is meeting. Each co-op has about 50 families at this point, representing a total of slightly less than 400 people for the two co-ops. My compadre, Mark, and I coordinate #1; Jackie and Fay still coordinate #2. Both have Steering Committees elected by the total membership.

We have two food sources: the Atlanta Community Food Bank, and Terra Verde Farms, a vendor at the Georgia State Farmers' Market. Terra Verde sells produce to us at cost, which is a great blessing.

On Tuesdays, Mark calls in the order for produce for our co-op meeting, and on Wednesday morning, one of our church members, Art Schiller, drives to the Farmers Market and picks up the produce and delivers it to the church. On Thursday mornings, Fay or I go to the Atlanta Community Food Bank, arriving before 6:00 as a rule, to pick a number which gives our shoppers a place in line when the Food Bank opens at 8:30. Going that early insures that we will get a good number and have a good choice of food for our people.

At 8:00, either Jackie and Paul McFatridge, with Richard Simmons driving our new truck (#2), or Mark with Willie Mae Williams (#1), head out to the Food Bank to be there to go in at 8:30. They shop, load the approximately one ton of food, and drive back to the church, arriving a little before 10:00, where our members are waiting to unload the truck. Tables have already been lined up and the food is placed on them. Empty boxes are lined up and members begin to fill the boxes according to sizes of families—single (1 to 3 people), double (4 to 7) or triple boxes (8 or more). All this takes about an hour, and meanwhile, some members of the co-op prepare snacks (usually pizza or sweets or both) for the moment when everybody's done with the work. It's really a festive time and a lot of fun as a rule (when things go smoothly). All members are responsible to pay $2.00 to join, to be present at each meeting, help do the work and get their food home. They also agree to either pay $2.00 each time we meet or find ways to compensate.

At about 11:00 we convene our meeting. Everyone gathers in a circle, we pray, sometimes sing, and have a devotional time unless we have a guest speaker. We ask who needs specific prayer and share news. After that we do business, make announcements, and hand out the boxes. We're done about 12:00. Then we clean up and everybody takes his or her box(es) and heads out. Typically, there are some boxes to be delivered to one or two shut-ins and there is the need to refrigerate food from boxes of members who could not be present. The next day, we give extra and unclaimed food as emergency food to whoever comes for it.

Our motto is "ask...seek...knock" from Jesus' words, recognizing that we depend on the Lord. The Lord has created a partnership of those who generously support our work—individuals, churches and foundations—and our members who work to do their part. Our members not only obtain needed food, they come together with others and develop a bit of a community, a sort of church, and they contribute and work together to make the co-op succeed. We look out for one another a little, pray for one another, visit when members are in the hospital or jail, etc., and have taken up offerings to send school supplies to Nicaragua.

I think the model is a good one; we've had more people coming to see what we do with an eye to starting food co-ops. You really do help make it happen, and I thank you.

May 1998

Dear Friends and Relatives:

With this letter I'm introducing you more fully to a person I've mentioned before, Kenny Redding. He is the new President of co-op #1. When I told him I wanted to write this letter about him, he gave permission and granted an interview.

Kenny is from South Georgia and will be 41 in a few days. He served in the Army in Germany and Alaska. He and his wife, Marilyn, have eleven children, eight of which are still at home. Due to an accident in which a forklift turned over on him in 1990, he walks with a pronounced limp. His doctors claim he must have surgery, but not before he gets his weight down. There are other difficulties, too: his wife is in and out of trouble because of addiction problems and one of his younger boys has been deaf since birth. Your prayers would be appreciated, as Kenny is taking him to Emory Hospital in early June for tests in the hopes that something may be done to help him.

Kenny is a person who knows something about poverty. His welfare income is $496/mo. The forklift job brought him nearly that much in a week; that was 8 years ago. Workman's compensation should have aided Kenny and taken care of the medical expenses. However, when ordered by the judge to take responsibility for the accident and pay Kenny $40,000, the recycle plant owner declared bankruptcy and transferred all property to others. The owner was subsequently jailed for trafficking in drugs, but he is now out and has reopened his recycle business. Kenny has never received a cent from the judgment or workmen's comp, nor have the medical bills been taken care of by it.

Kenny has good things to say about the difference the co-op has made to him. He was raised in the church, but he "didn't take it too seriously" until he came to the Georgia Avenue Food Co-op four years ago. He says the devotional times make him think and, among other things, he has become a better parent. He is close to his children, and his smallest child, Lissy, who is 5, always comes and gets him to make sure he says nighttime prayers with her. He prays with all the kids and they nearly always go to church. He says, "The co-op took me out of the streets; I'm not out there wasting my time anymore." "The food really make (sic) a difference—boy, do it!" are his words, but that's not the main thing for him. He enjoys being here, around the church, and when he is doing his extra job of handing out the leftover food, it makes him think of Jesus feeding the five thousand.

Kenny has gone to Nicaragua twice now, and loved it. Everybody liked him, too; not just the people who went on the trip, but the Nicaraguans. It's common when contact is made with folks there for someone to say, "Tell Kenny hello for me." He's not going back this year, but by the grace of God will again, and I expect Kenny and the two who are going this year to form a committee to continue to work at this Nicaraguan connection.

He's going to South Georgia this long weekend and will visit, among others, his 97-year-old great grandmother. Kenny knows little about his family history; I encouraged him to take advantage of this woman's knowledge. She is surely a storehouse of wisdom and information—she may have knowledge of slavery days and even African connections! It would be a shame to let all that pass with her when her mind is still sharp and she is so willing to talk.

Kenny brings a lot of good sense to his new position: he has a firm but gentle way of quashing arguments and works toward reconciliation; he doesn't start quarrels or try to boss people around and he's not one to sing his own praises. Kenny looks out for others and tries to choose his words carefully. When he gets wind of rumors or people try to draw him into gossipy cliques, he gently puts a stop to it. He is part of the black community in a way that I am not; he had a lot to inform me about things he hears and sees, and, as we talked, I grew more and more sure that the Lord had gifted us by placing Kenny in this position. It's a blessing to have someone who is trustworthy and wants to ensure that the Lord's work is done in the co-op.

Kenny's situation is not one I'd want to be in, but it is great to be in a work that makes a contribution toward keeping him going. He in turn is a gift toward keeping this work developing and helps to keep me going, too (as do you, and I thank you).


July 1998


Dear Friends and Relatives:
Last Thursday was a rough day.

To start with, I had a message to call Jimmy, one of our folks slated to make the trip to Nicaragua. I called: "Rev. Chad, I'm not going to Nicaragua." He didn't feel prepared adequately with vaccines, and he wasn't going. I could tell pretty quickly there was no changing his mind, so with little resistance, I said, "OK," but it was a blow.

Then Sarah, the primary coordinator of the trip, called: "Where is Ella (the other person going to Nicaragua)? She was supposed to meet me here at 9:00." (at that point it was 10:00—Sarah was waiting at the health center). I said I'd call and see if I could reach her. No answer. But 20 minutes later Ella called from home. "Rev. Chad, I'm not going to Nicaragua." She, with Jimmy, had decided the health preparations were inadequate and she couldn't take the risk. This is a week and a day before the trip. I had been so sure everything was really going well this time—we had gotten the passports in such timely fashion; the preparation committee had been meeting regularly.... I was feeling low.

Then, later in the day, "R" came by the church drunk, wanting a voucher to get a change of clothes from the Family Store across the street. I said, "No," but that there were some shirts in the office I'd get for him. He followed me, standing behind me as I unlocked the door. (We have to keep our doors locked all the time.) The shirts were near Mark's desk. I got them for him and off he went. I headed home to work at my home office.

I wasn't there long when the phone rang. Mark was distraught: "I can't find my blue pouch anywhere!" The blue pouch is Mark's corral for money, checks, bills, all the stuff he has to haul back and forth and keep track of. Plus, Mark was already frantically trying to get things wrapped up to leave town. I said I'd be right back. On the way, it hit me—"R!" I had turned my back on him to get the shirts, which he must have then used to hide the pouch.

I began to comb the neighborhood, starting with his living place, an "abandoned" house. (What a hole—no one should live that way!) I headed up toward some of the seedier areas of Summerhill and began asking for R. Yes, they had spotted him. I cruised and looked. Went by his mother's. Gave up. Went home. But before I went home, I let the neighborhood guys know we'd give $50 to anybody that came up with it. The matter got more urgent to them!

I hadn't been back long when the doorbell rang. There stood Kiwi and LaKing (one of Hawk's sons), puffing hard from running: "We just spotted him but we've got to hurry." I took the two guys and off we went. He was gone. "He can't be far—it was just 7 or 8 minutes ago." We searched and looked and gave up again.

Once again, I hadn't been back long when the doorbell rang. This time it was "M" and his girlfriend: "We had him in the car and he gave me this (—one of the checks Mark had written to send with our folks to Nicaragua). He's got the blue pouch, carrying it under his arm. I tried to bring him to you, but he made me let him out. I'll show you where."

Off we went. I was praying "Lord, please help us" the whole time, because I didn't want my partner to have to deal with all the problems attendant upon having that pouch gone—checks to be stopped, accounts closed (?), bills that would need to be obtained a second time, who knows what all! The money was the least of our concern.

We cruised and looked. Went into another abandoned house. No luck. But we kept coming back to that spot, and the third time the girl said, "He's in there—I saw somebody peeking out the window." His mother showed up right then, too, walking. I stopped the truck and started up the steps. Out he came, still high. "R, where's the pouch? I need that pouch." "It's in the bushes—they threw it out there?" (They?!) The privet was high, yard unkempt. We searched in the bushes and found it, none of the money but most of the papers and checks still there.

I'm not sure Mark's ever been so glad to see me. We lost about $120 (our co-op contributions and petty cash) and had to cancel one book of checks, but we *think* we have everything else. Actually, riding around looking for R was a bit of an adventure and drew me a little closer to some of my neighbors. They were tickled to be rewarded, but it was more than that—they felt good about helping us at the church. Now, I need to work out restitution matters with R—he, too, is still our neighbor, and I don't think jail's the answer.

Others have come forward to take Jimmy and Ella's

place, not from our co-op, but from other churches. In the end, even for Thursday, I am left thankful.

### August 1998

Dear Friends and Relatives:

This young woman has had an unbelievable life. Yet she has lived right here in the city, a few blocks from me and has been my neighbor the whole time I've been here.

Her family came out of Appalachia. Her father worked hard here in a rock quarry. He had to go to the doctor last year and was terrified, as he had never been to a doctor in his life. He is 75 years old.

The young woman, I will call her "Dee," came to me at the church about 5 years ago now. She said she didn't know how to live, and she wanted to have life.

Growing up, her brother tried to molest her. At one point, at the worst, she called the police to charge him with attempted rape. Her parents got angry at her.

She got involved at age 15 with a Mexican boy, who at first seemed nice enough. But he became very possessive, and finally, psychotic in his jealousy and evil. They had four children together by the time she was 20—they never were married and she was afraid to try to get away from him. He was finally sent to jail for beating one of the baby twin girls, which gave her a chance to get away; she found a new boyfriend. When the jailed former boyfriend was released, a quick list of his pursuit of her includes abducting and raping her, chasing her on the road when she was driving her new boyfriend's car and ramming the car with his until hers was totaled, and finally stalking her and the new boyfriend with a gun, and killing the only person he found in their apartment, shooting him in his sleep in cold blood, for which he is serving a too-short jail sentence. He told their children a couple of years ago when they came to visit him in jail to tell Dee that when he got out he would find her and "hold her head in the toilet 'til she drowned." During all the abuse and craziness, her parents did nothing.

In 1994, she got to the place where she was so anxiety ridden and fearful, she thought she was "going to die." She ran out of the house one night in her fear and ended up at the next-door neighbor's, saying she needed to go to Grady Hospital because she was sick. This woman was a Christian, a black woman, who wisely said she didn't need to go to the hospital for her sickness, but to Jesus. Dee prayed to Jesus, and immediately received a sense of peace. It was soon after that that she came to see me; she told me she came to the church because she didn't know how to live. She was baptized in the church, and has been a member of the church ever since.

Dee has not been able to live with and raise the four children as her new boyfriend, now husband, does not want them to be around, reminding him of her past, and he is also afraid they will tell the jailed father where they live. (They live with the fear of this psycho's release, which we thought was going to be this last March, but parole was denied. I and others in the church wrote letters and prayed against his release.) Of course, this has created even more problems. The oldest of her children, a boy of 16, is now becoming more like his jailed father. So the children, all four of them (she also has a fifth child with her husband), have lived with Dee's mother, along with several other sisters of hers, who also have children. (It is an unbelievable, indescribable situation.) Now Dee finds herself afraid of her pot-smoking, more-and-more-violent-talking son, which distresses her. Dee's oldest girl is 14 and pregnant, also by a Mexican boy. Dee is angry and distressed by this, and has gone to the police to have the 22-year old boyfriend arrested, doing what she can at this point to keep her daughters from repeating her story. The police have done nothing at all. She makes an effort to give the daughter love and support which she never got from her mother, taking her to doctor's appointments, etc.

She needs your prayers. Dee does have life now; she is learning to live. She is making major breaks with the ways she has been raised (neglected!). Her family doesn't understand her and her new faith and ways, which is also painful. It's a privilege to be with her as she struggles, though I have to say, sometime the struggles are overwhelming to hear, let alone to live (and I have not told you the half of them in this letter!).

As always, I continue with thankfulness in this place and gratefulness to you for your kind support of me. As you know, I am not very thoughtful about writing notes, etc., for which I ask forgiveness. Bear with me, please.


October 1998

Dear Friends and Relatives:

L was born in the Bronx in 1951 to a mother who was 13 years of age. He never knew his father. He grew up there, raised by his great grandmother and his great aunt. He started drinking peach brandy and wine when he was 12. By the 8th grade, marijuana had become his favorite drug choice. He went into the Army when he was 17 because he was "headed for trouble," and was shipped to Vietnam. He became a serious heroin addict in Vietnam—drugs were everywhere, cheap, high grade and easy to obtain. He was busted in the Army for drugs, but managed to avoid a dishonorable discharge on a technicality.

Drugs were a lifelong habit, as well as doing what it took, including theft or embezzlement, to pay for the habit. When he got out of the Army and went back to New York, he started selling drugs. He was arrested in 1971 and put into a rehab program, but even then never quit smoking pot.

As a child, his great grandmother made him go to church. When he got to age 13, he would dress up to go but then duck out and do other things. Nevertheless, he had the influence of the church and his great grandmother and her old-fashioned ways.

He moved to Georgia in 1980, and soon after arriving moved into our area. He was using pot and more alcohol by this time, and even though he would get jobs, he was always under the influence of something. He would start off the morning at 6:30 or 7:00 before work with 1/2 joint and 1/2 pint of wine, and finish it on and off during the morning. On the way home he would get a quart of beer and another joint. Obviously, he couldn't stay on a job long this way, what with the accidents, thievery, etc.

He married in 1983, but stayed mired in his addictions. In 1987 he heard there was a service going on at

Georgia Avenue Church on Wednesdays and he started coming up here. In 1990 he was tossed in jail again on traffic violations, and something about that began to make him think. He and his wife had had to take two of her grandchildren who were 3 and 5 into their home, which didn't make him happy, but when he talked to those grandchildren from jail he cried, knowing he wasn't setting a good example for them. Nevertheless, when released he resumed his old habits. But a few months after getting out, he finally prayed; he finally turned to God, and asked God to help him. He entered a detox program and has been sober since the first day. He also began to faithfully attend the AA meetings we have here on Thursday and Saturday nights.

Our little services played a role in drawing L to God. He says, "When I think of Georgia Avenue and of Fay (who nearly always leads our little services), it gave me a place to come where I felt at peace." People here seemed to understand his struggles and weren't looking down on him and condemning and judging him. The services were always "supportive and motivational" for him, and he "felt proud when I could say on Wednesdays 'I'm going to the church'—those services did a lot for me."

L hasn't been around too much, because he got a steady job and has been working for five years. He joined a church and has become a deacon. Unfortunately, recently he's had problems with arthritis such that he has had to have surgery and cannot do his regular job. The good news part of that is that now he can come to Georgia Avenue on Wednesdays. It's been good to have him back—it's great to hear him pray and tell his story, which he does eloquently. He says he wants to come here every time he can, because he wants to give something back "because [Georgia Avenue] gave so much to me."

Many factors went into this man being rescued: his great grandmother's example and values; church in his early years; a faithful wife that loves him and hung on; his wife's grandchildren; jail; our Georgia Avenue Wednesday services, and on and on. L often wears a T-shirt that says on it, "Loose that man and let him go." L has been loosed. It's a blessing to be part of the mix used of God to loose him, and a joy to see him freed from chains that bound him for so long. God is good. Our God reigns!

Thank you for your thoughtfulness and support of me, too.

November, December 1998

Dear Friends and Relatives:

Obviously I am very late with this November letter, so it'll be for December, too.

Some of the neighbors around our church building are not too happy with us. They think that reaching out to people in need creates trouble. The neighbors on the west are angry, saying we trash the place and invite thieves to our building. Their home and cars have been broken into several times. They have moved and rent the house out now. They've really been on the warpath this past week, coming in and yelling at Mark and me. "Why don't you only invite in the deserving ones? The undeserving don't merit one bit of your attention!" Our neighbor across the street on the east is questioning whether we should have our meal and our food co-ops. She, too, has experienced theft and break-ins of her car. I find it hard to believe that this woman, who is black and who not that long ago couldn't have bought into our neighborhood because of her race, is so ready to ban others—and she is vocal about being Christian. Our neighbor on the north is one of the officers of the neighborhood association. I think it would be fair to say that he and most of the association place high priority on raising property values and fighting crime. They don't seem too concerned about diversity and those in need; these are not neighbors they want to have anything to do with. We (our co-op members) invited him and the other officers of that association to a dinner so we could get acquainted and let them know what we are doing. He said "no"—if we want to inform them about our work, come to the regular meeting and make a presentation. That's an invitation I think we'll pass up, at least for now. It would be rather like going into a lions' den to focus their hostilities squarely on us.

Of course, we didn't invent crime or bring it into our neighborhood; conditions that breed poverty and crime are some of the reasons I came here. Summerhill and other poor neighborhoods surround increasingly affluent Grant Park. Whether I do anything or not, the "undeserving" are going to keep making forays into the area. And I'll be honest with you—for the most part, I can't tell the "deserving" from the "undeserving"; all of them are people, my neighbors, who live in this area. So, do we quit caring for everyone so we can keep the "undeserving" away? We have redoubled our efforts to make sure our people are not throwing down trash after our Wednesday meal. The crime is not OK, for sure, but we're not responsible for it; in fact, I would like to think we are working in our own way to stop it. Several alcoholics and drug dealers have been converted; some who were thieves are no longer; and we provide for people so they don't need to steal.

I admit the problems get to me sometime, too; I have no magical immunity from them. My wheelbarrow was stolen last week, the hubcaps from the car two nights ago, our trash herbie's been stolen twice, our home was broken into, our cars have been broken into. And there are other concerns.

I'm sure if I said, "Lord, I've had it and I'm leaving," I could do that. But I'm just as sure I'm where I'm "supposed" to be. However, I don't want to live here and have a holier-than-thou attitude toward my more affluent neighbors. We'll have to keep looking for ways to build bridges to at least some of these folks.

I have to say, though, sometimes it seems that at least an aspect of "the problem" is not the people who are poor, but people who think they know who are the "deserving" and the "undeserving." Who of us is "deserving?" What does that mean? Do the scriptures say, "Love your *deserving* neighbor as yourself?" I see little movement among the more advantaged residents to get to know neighbors of poverty and color and their concerns and needs and to be neighbors to them. What's more, there is a readiness to see those of us who do as some sort of "enemy." None of this exempts me from the command to love these neighbors, too, but it's a bit of a test at times.

I have two requests with which I need help. One of the persons on this mailing list, a friend in his 50s who has been very supportive of this ministry, has been diagnosed with a form of "incurable cancer." He is married and has two children. He has gone from robust to emaciated almost overnight. Please pray for him and his family.

Secondly, Fay's car is beyond repair, or at least beyond her ability to pay to repair. If any of you have a car you would be willing to donate, she is in need of wheels (automatic, preferably station wagon or van, but whatever).

May this coming season be a blessed one for you. I am ever so thankful for your ongoing prayers and financial support, and very much aware of what a gift you are to me.

Monday morning at 7:30 a.m. my doorbell rang. Monday is my day off and I was sleeping late after being up late the night before. I put on my robe and went down to find C there, all decked out in his new sweat suit, toboggan cap and sunglasses, happy as could be that he had new stuff. C is mentally incompetent—at this point, he seems gentle as a lamb, but he has a long arrest record including rape and assault of various kinds, and I am told he murdered his grandmother. So, he has been in prison the last decade. He needs to be in some sort of group home but he is not, and he has sort of cast himself on me. He is totally alone, subject to being beat up for his money, and needing someone to be his SSI payee. I quite frankly am not open to being his payee. It is soooo much hassle! Furthermore, he's out there not being supervised about taking his medications, which is scary, too. The best I could get him to do for the moment was to give me a hundred dollars of the three hundred that his present payee gave him (I don't know if he was being ripped off or not, but the payee can't stand to deal with him any more), so that he couldn't blow all of his money and if robbed not lose it all.

When he arrived at my door Monday, he was so tickled with all of his purchases. In two days he had spent all of the $200, so he came to get the last $100, which I gave him. He gave me a watch to keep for him—he had bought it, but can't wear it, as it will be something for which he will be jumped. Why did he spend his money to buy it?! He most definitely doesn't have my mindset—I had tried to dissuade him from making that specific purchase so he'd have money for food and shelter. My counsel did absolutely no good. I'm sure by now that he has no more money and, as of this writing, there are still 10 days left in the month.

I'm not comfortable keeping C in my home. There are too many unknowns about him for me. He's a big guy, too. But I'm afraid if he's not already, he will soon be on the street again. That's painful to consider given that it is beginning to get pretty cool at nights.


January 1999

Dear Friends and Relatives:

"If you have come to help me, you are wasting your time. But if you've come because your liberation is bound up with mine, we can work together." –Lilah Watson

Some members of our church and a few co-op members went with me to Columbia Theological Seminary to a one-day seminar on servant leadership. Diana Chambers, who has been a part of the Servant Leadership School, which is related to Church of the Savior in Washington, DC, led the seminar. When my co-op people heard the quote above, they jumped right on it. They asked her to repeat it a couple of times, so they could write it down.

It's not usual for people like those in our co-ops to be at classes at places like Columbia. I was a little concerned about how the class would be approached, because it is true that a number of us are not used to "academic erudition." Furthermore, these settings are for "haves," where it is easy to talk about "being with the poor," etc. and what "they" need, but of course, some of my group were the "they." The only other people we encountered like my co-op people were working in the dining hall. But Diana was obviously comfortable with everyone, and approached issues common to our lives in a mostly down-to-earth way. It was a good experience for us.

Where is the Lord leading us with these co-ops? Ms. Watson's quote has something to do with it. I do know our people get food they need, and I know that it is more than just physical food, as important as that is. We go to classes together, we share together our woes and joys, and we do so in the name of Jesus. One of the members of co-op #2, Edna Dillard, died this week of cancer. Fay ministered to her so beautifully. Edna's daughter has contacted Fay and asked her to be on the program at Edna's funeral. The daughter, whom I do not know, says that her mother thought so much of Fay and was always talking about her, and she just thought Fay ought to be there. Fay said she would. Edna was black, Fay is white. Our people model a kind of wonderful racial harmony. Anyway, wherever the Lord is leading us, he is leading us to relate, and to form a little bit of community together, and thereby liberating us.

One of the participants at the seminar said that his church had begun some years earlier to create space for homeless people. He said that the first thing that the church members learned that amazed them was "these people were just like us." I'm grateful for their ministry, but I also reacted emotionally. What were the church members thinking before? Where does this come from, this sense that "they" are *not* like "us"?! What a huge barrier between peoples! That barrier is powerful and has a very real effect to keep people oppressed, homeless, in jail, apart, at war, etc. How would "they" be different—three legs, elephant hide? Of course, some continually try, even now, to conjure up such differences, holding that certain ones are not as moral, have smaller brains, are not as worthy, whatever. Toward what end? Whom do these definitions benefit? The ones who believe "they" are different are really saying "we" are different—better—and are justified staying apart, building fences, protecting our comfort in any fashion, etc. It is a jolt then when some are led by God to learn that "they," too, are human just as I am human, "they," too, hurt and get hungry and feel pain, etc. Truly learning that, however, is liberating to all parties.

A pastor I know in an affluent area of Atlanta told me that a homeless man had come to the church at Advent and had joined the church. The church is in an uproar! His words are, "It's kicking our butt!" This "least-of-these" is a member they don't want but can't turn away and who's not leaving. No one seems to know how to treat him: some are handing him money; they are uncomfortable with giving him the church directory, which is part of their membership ritual, since he will know where the other members live; apparently, no one has invited him into their home. The man cannot be met and related to as a human being. The Lord came at Advent in this poor black man to this wealthy white church. Sometime it's uncomfortable to have God come to liberate us.

I think Lilah Watson is saying we *all* need freedom, not just "they" and it doesn't come from *helping*. *You* don't have *it* to give to me; it's about us together. Those who have can make contributions to the lives of those who have not, but it is just as true that those who have not can make contributions to the liberation of those who have, who may not even know that they are captive. Liberation is about *knowing* "them" and learning they are "just like us."


February 1999

Dear Friends and Relatives:

Mark, my associate, and I have begun a class on what we call "servant leadership" with members of the co-ops who have committed themselves to being present. As we planned, we began to focus more on the word "ownership." We have thought of the co-ops as a ministry of "mercy" (food), a ministry of evangelism and discipleship (formed in the name of the Lord with regular devotion times), community building (people coming together regularly for a good reason), and self-development (individuals members having responsibilities and privileges and therefore, to a degree, each an owner). But there are gaps to overcome. Mark and I still have the major responsibility for keeping the whole thing afloat, and it is still easy for the regular members to defer to us, even though there is a lot of respect and mutual camaraderie. In any case, we believe that a sense of ownership is key to the future, not just of the co-ops, but for whatever else may develop out of the community ministry. But as we planned for the class, we realized that that sense of ownership needs to be strengthened if our members are to truly take leadership.

So, we thought, what if Chad and Mark weren't here? That would definitely force a shift regarding ownership, power and leadership. So two classes ago we gave people the following "news article" and asked them to think about some questions we attached.

### "Two Local Church Community Workers Killed in Truck Wreck"

Tuesday afternoon the Rev. Chad Hale and his co-worker, Mr. Mark Jordan, were killed as they were driving north on Old National Highway when a semi-trailer ran a red light, hitting their truck directly and smashing into three other cars passing through the intersection. There were no other fatalities, though 4 other people were taken to South Fulton Hospital, where one of them is still in critical condition.

The Rev. Hale and Mr. Jordan were in the truck owned by the Georgia Avenue Food Cooperative for which they were co-directors. The cooperative is located in Grant Park at the Georgia Avenue Church building, where Rev. Hale has been the pastor since 1981.

The semi-trailer driver was uninjured. He apparently had been driving for nearly twenty hours straight, which is illegal, and blacked out as he was approaching the intersection with the low sun directly in his eyes. He has been detained and charged with vehicular homicide.

The Rev. Hale is survived by his wife, Barbara Antonoplos, and four children, and Mr. Jordan by his wife, Joanne Jordan, and one child, Joseph, aged 4. A joint funeral service will be held on Monday, Feb. 3, at the Georgia Avenue Church."

(Actually, it was a little odd writing about my own death! I'm the one who had the responsibility to write the article.)

It was Mark's role to be the discussion leader, and it was very interesting. Our co-op members "got into it."

But what was most interesting to Mark and me was that it became clear this exercise wasn't just for *them*, it was for *Mark and Chad!* It became evident that we haven't done nearly as good a job being "servant leaders" as we thought we had. When we really looked at the situation with a view to our sudden absence, we realized our co-op members would not be in a good position to continue the co-ops. It was an eye-opening exercise; the Spirit became the Teacher so that *all of us* would learn more about servant leadership.

Now we have to take seriously what we realized last week, and, by the grace of God, we will. We'd appreciate your prayers in this regard. We're not sure how, but we're committed to the journey.

## March 1999

Dear Friends and Relatives:

A filming crew approached us recently about using our church as one of the sites for a TV miniseries. Whether it will work out I don't know, but they like our sanctuary and it looks like they will follow up with us. It will be for a series based on Taylor Branch's book, *Parting the Waters*, which is exciting to us.

It puts me in mind of the last time we got into something like this. That was a trip! "Robocop 3" producers approached us about using our building for a movie about an abandoned church that had become a home for urban homeless people. We weren't saying yes, and we weren't saying no. They talked in terms of paying us six or seven thousand dollars. They were talking big about all the money they had to throw around.

We were in a situation of financial need, as we had leaks in our roof and no money for a new one. But money doesn't drive our decisions—doing the Lord's will, or at least trying, is of more interest to us. When it became a serious matter that the studio wanted to use our building, we had to decide whether we really would be willing for them to do so. I wasn't against it, but some were because the film would have violence in it, and they didn't want to be appearing to condone such. I thought it might be a way the

Lord would provide for us, but I didn't feel strongly about it.

So, we asked the church that shares our building with us, Southwest Christian Fellowship, how they felt about it. I did feel strongly that if anyone was going to leave because of the movie, it wasn't worth it. Southwest wasn't for it, but said their feeling wasn't so strong that they would leave if we did it.

The filmmakers came to a place of saying, "Yes, we definitely want to use your space and we need an answer by Sunday night." We had a social gathering for our church planned that Sunday night at my home. The timing was beautiful; we ended up spending a good bit of the time debating whether to go with this movie thing. Most people were for it, a few were not. We asked those who were not if they felt so strongly about it that it would affect their place in the church. All said "no," if we decided to go with it, they weren't going to leave. If anybody felt that strongly about it, that would decide the issue—no money is important enough to divide our fellowship.

We weren't comfortable, though, making the decision by majority rule. We know it is easy to fool ourselves when it comes to money, plus we knew that there was potential for a big mess with all that the filmmakers were planning to do (make the sanctuary into a "catholic-like" space, paint our white walls maroon, build in a huge pulpit area, move in large statues of Mary, etc.; it would be a big production and disruptive!). So, we also needed a clear "yes" from the Lord!

But how do you discern the Lord's mind on the spur of the moment for something that's not clear? We decided we would use the Old Testament "Urim and Thummin" method, or as the disciples did to replace Judas, we would cast lots. In our case, we translated casting lots into flipping a coin! We would flip the coin twice: two heads would be "yes," two tails would be "no" and head and tail would mean "you guys can decide this on your own." These were the options we set up, then we prayed, and I flipped a quarter—two heads!

After we flipped the coin, I asked the church for permission to negotiate with the filmmakers. When they called that night, I said we wanted to have the sanctuary repainted plus $20,000! The man said, "You're out of your mind—they'll never go for that." I said "fine." But the next day, they came back offering $16,000 and the repainting, and we took it. By the time they finished, we had made nearly $23,000, we got a new roof, and a sanctuary that looked like new. "Robocop 3" was never shown in theaters, only on video! It worked out beautifully and provided some entertainment to boot.

That episode was so much fun; it's not one I'll forget. The key to it was that we were free, wanted to honor all involved and wanted the Lord's will to be done. We weren't hooked by their offer of money—we thought if the offer was provision from the Lord, he would see it through, and if it wasn't, we didn't want it. Above all, we didn't want the church divided.

I am always in your debt. I am so grateful to you for your interest, prayers, and in some cases, financial aid. Your support is a great blessing to me.

April 1999

Dear Friends and Relatives:

My letter will be a little shorter this time. Once again, I have come to the end of the month and still not gotten this letter to you.

Rob Johnson, Chief Operating Officer of the Atlanta Community Food Bank, is going to begin today (Wednesday) to lead our co-op leadership group through a process of shaping and forming the new third food co-op. Such an approach will insure that the ones who will lead the co-op, plus a few other co-op members, will be in on the ground floor of forming the co-op, which is, in my view, very important. Chad, or Chad and Mark, will not be dictating how this co-op will look—we will work it out together with Rob's leadership. I don't know that it will be much different from the present ones, but it might.

We did not know for sure how to pick the new leaders and this has had Mark and me buffaloed for a while, since it is such an important issue. We ended up deciding to proceed as follows. We have been wanting to begin the leadership classes, which I wrote about previously when I scared a few of you (my apologies) with the article about Mark and me being killed in a truck wreck. But along with teaching about leadership, we had a secret agenda: find new leaders for the third food co-op. We knew that if we just announced, "Whoever would like to lead the new food co-op (a part-time paid position), come to this class" we would have a lot of people who weren't so interested in serving others as being paid. We couldn't figure out how we would then ferret out the right leaders. So, we decided to go ahead with the class to teach about servant leadership, but not to announce that we were also searching for the new co-op leaders.

Six people began the class along with Mark and me. Three people have been able and willing to hang in there faithfully: Lucille Reese, Ella Duffy and Kenny Redding. Lucille has made it clear in the course of our classes that she does not see herself as an active leader (though she does lead, in her own way, through her faithfulness and dependability); that left Ella, from co-op #2, and Kenny, from co-op #1. So Mark and I approached them, told them what we had in mind, and asked them to pray about and consider leading the new co-op. They spent time doing so and have responded in the positive.

So, now begins the new phase of our class with Rob, a gifted "outsider" coming in to lead all of us in this "co-op formation stage." I am grateful to Rob; he has been a faithful friend of our co-ops since joining the Advisory Committee several years ago to work with us. I would very much appreciate your prayers as we enter this work now.


May 1999

Dear Friends and Relatives:

My good friend and brother in Christ, Roland Steinlin, died (was "promoted to glory" as his wife Judy, who was in the Salvation Army, says) earlier this month. Roland lived in Columbia, SC, with his wife and two children. He had stomach cancer and suffered greatly before the end.

I want to recognize Roland because he was instrumental in making it possible for me to continue to work with people of need in this area. When I found myself in the position of having to seek a new direction, an aspect of which was to ascertain whether there was financial backing "out there," Roland's generous financial response was the key in the lock to let me know that the Lord was making a way for me to pursue this new phase of ministry. I am very grateful to him and to Judy, as they continued to be strong supporters of this work right up until he died. Many people have been fed in many ways, and not just here in my work, by Roland's faith and generosity. He was a gift of God to me and to many.

We are continuing to have fruitful meetings to plan for the new co-op 3. Rob Johnson is providing good leadership; there are presently six of us "being led."

Many of the programs that are set up to "help poor people" have buried within them certain assumptions that are harmful to the people they are set up to "help." One of the most harmful assumptions is that people in need have nothing to offer. The dynamic of the "helping" makes the "helper" a sort of hero, and the person being helped ends up with a bad taste in his/her mouth, and maybe having a hard time understanding why, since after all, he/she was helped and everybody was so nice. But the relationship is an unequal one that unconsciously feeds off of the need.

While we in the Georgia Avenue Community Ministry do not begin with the assumption that our people do not have gifts and talents to offer, the "helping dynamic" is difficult to change. It's not just programs or other people that cause the problems: it is me. After all, I am the director; I am a pastor; I am middle class; I have many years of education; I am used to being in charge (while the co-op members are used to having someone else in charge); and I am white. I am used to reading, writing, having meetings, discussions. It is "obvious" in meeting settings that I have much to offer; the co-op members have little. The power is mostly on my side. They know this, too, and they generally start out much quieter; I start out talking, "priming the pump." It is difficult for me to shut up and sit in the awkward silence waiting for someone else to speak; difficult for them, too, and they often expect me to rescue us all from the awkwardness. After all, we're all agreed I have so much to offer. Eugene Peterson, writing about the vocation of pastoring, describes what happens in this way: "But something subtle is going on.... When I am helping others, I am stronger and they are weaker; I am competent in relation to their incompetence; they are thanking, praising, admiring while I am being gracious, understanding, and merciful.... It is a good feeling. It is also addictive and so I seek out occasions and people in which it can be reinforced. At some point along the way I cross a line—my messianic work takes center stage and Messiah is pushed to the sidelines." (*Under the Unpredictable Plant*, p.179)

Seeing this dynamic, we set up our co-op 3 planning meetings so that I am not leading, but Rob is, and Mark and I are among the participants. That arrangement aids us to act together on a more equal footing. My goal is to collaborate with my brother and sister members in the co-ops, as opposed to helping them. Rob is doing a fine job leading the group; I am learning to listen and hold my counsel; the co-op members are speaking up more. We are learning together, forming new relationships, and all of us are using our gifts in the process.

The co-op planning group met the same afternoon that I was away at Roland's memorial service. In my absence, they formulated this mission statement:

*The mission of co-op #3 is to create in the name of the Lord a membership community of up to 50 households (close to or connected to Georgia Avenue Church) that gives members a sense of extended family and the opportunity to work together to provide supplemental nourishment (tummy and soul) so that no **body** is hungry.*

I *like* it—all the more because I wasn't present to help write it! It's fitting that it was formulated even as Roland was being honored, and to my mind, adds to that honor.

June 1999

Dear Friends and Relatives:

This letter is about Kenny and Ella, the two coordinators of our future co-op #3.

Kenny lives in Cabbagetown, three blocks from the now famous textile mill fire/rescue that was on national TV last month. The man who lives across the street from him came to Kenny at the first of June and told him he had bought Kenny's house and gave him 30 days to move. Kenny has eleven children, eight of which are still at home, and has lived in the house for nine years and always paid his rent on time. The landlord did not tell him he was planning to sell the house or notify him when he had sold the house. He was informed by the new owner, who had been a seemingly friendly neighbor prior to this. Kenny asked him to give him more time, which he refused.

Kenny asked the landlord why he didn't tell him he was planning to sell the house and at least ask Kenny if he would want to buy it. The landlord said he thought Kenny was too poor to buy it, and mumbled excuses for the lack of communication. He basically said, "You're going to have to live with it."

What makes this more difficult is that Kenny had major surgery scheduled for June 14, which, according to the physicians, could not be put off. So, he's in the hospital and the doctor has told him he will be in the hospital at least through the end of this thirty-day period. I asked him, lying there in the bed, if he was really worried about his need to move, but he said the Lord had really given him peace about it. He is confident the Lord is going to work it out.

I contacted a friend of mine who is a lawyer who tells me that legally Kenny must be given 60 days' notice. So far, I've had no luck contacting the new owner by phone, so I left a letter in his mailbox today.

Rob, who is leading the co-op #3 planning meetings, has faithfully brought a flip chart to all our meetings, as we do not have one at the church. It's heavy duty plastic and looks as if it could withstand a nuclear blast.

At one of our meetings, Rob offered the flip chart as a gift to Co-op #3, a first gift for the new co-op. But he didn't just give it—he asked if we wanted it and made the issue about accepting the chart an aspect of the class discussion. Did we want it and how would we make the decision? Where would it be stored and who would take responsibility for it? How would the new co-op take care of its possessions?

This may seem like a trivial subject, and an obvious decision. But I was impressed with Rob's wisdom: he didn't presume on us, plus the issue became grist for the learning process.

We agreed by consensus that it would be an asset to have the flip chart. Co-op #3 would have something of its own even before it's off the ground! We decided where to store it, and Rob showed us how to work the rather fancy gizmo, which has to be "manhandled" a certain way.

But then Ella said, "I don't think we should just keep it to ourselves. We need to share this with the other co-ops!"

If owning something new and fancy is a good way to begin, having a spirit of willingness to share and cooperate is even better. I think our new co-op is in good hands.


### July 1999

Dear Friends and Relatives:

I just turned 54 a few days ago. Age has never been a big issue with me, but I was with one of our church members recently on her birthday, and she said, "You know, it won't be too long before we're sixty!" Wow! That hit me! 60! Me!! I haven't even grown up yet!

Regarding last month's letter and Kenny's need to move: the landlord called the day I mailed my last letter to you. Finally, he communicated, via phone. When I took the receiver, he said, "I consulted with my lawyer and he said to tell you not to set foot on any of my properties," and he hung up!

I didn't know what to think of that. I called Kenny, who said the landlord had called him at the hospital and told Kenny he didn't want anybody else knowing about his business. Kenny told him to call me and tell me himself if he didn't want me in his business. You know, in the church, an individual is not just alone—if the landlord is going to deal with Kenny, then he has to deal with Kenny's "family" in the church (I'm using "church" here loosely given that we're in the co-op together). The landlord also asked him, "How much time are you talking about?" clearly backing off the requirement for Kenny to be out by June 30. If Kenny weren't connected with others, what would the landlord have tried to do? Apparently, he thought he could bully a poor man. Would he have come and thrown Kenny's stuff out on the street himself? He didn't like it when he discovered he had other folks to deal with.

It started when one of our co-op members asked us to pray for her husband who was in the hospital. Innocent enough. We missed him, but didn't realize all that was going on.

The husband is on disability because of a fall he took which was the cause of headaches and memory loss. Recently, because of headaches, he went back to the clinic in which all the original medical exam work was done, though he hadn't been back for several years. They acted strange, saying they couldn't do the scheduled tests that day and rescheduled his appointment. He said to himself, "What tests?"

In the meantime, he went to Grady, where he learned his blood pressure was high and that he had an infection, for which they gave him antibiotics. He decided to keep his second appointment at the other place, though he considered not going since he was feeling better. Again the behavior of the staff was strange. They took his picture, had him sign papers advising him of his rights; when he wanted to go to the restroom, they insisted that he use the staff one at hand; and they kept him locked in the building. They called for an ambulance to take him somewhere. One of the staff members let him out when he said he needed some air, and he was able to get to his car and drive himself home.

That night, two Fulton County sheriffs came to his

home. He invited them in, and they said he needed to go with them. They wouldn't explain why or where. They didn't want him to reach into his pockets, and when he said he was going to get his shoes, they said no. He told his wife to get his shoes for him. "You won't need shoes where you're going!" they said. Won't need shoes!! He agreed to go with them, as he judged they were keyed up to use force and he didn't want to give them any excuse for that. They took him to a local mental hospital where he was admitted. Still he was not told why, but "psychosis" was written on his admission papers. (All this is from going to the clinic about his headaches!)

Finally, a nurse who came in at 11:00 p.m. said, "You need to be more careful." He said, "What are you talking about?" "Well, you drew a gun on your wife and beat her, didn't you?" My friend was flabbergasted: "No ma'am! We've been married for 26 years and nothing like that ever happened!" The next day when the doctor came to see him and asked about the same incidents, he said, "Of course not! What is this all about?!" The doctor asked him if he could talk to his wife. My friend dialed her and handed him the phone. She said no such incidents had ever occurred.

The doctor eventually agreed that something had gone wrong, though they kept him all that day and night and released him the next morning, July 1. He did not take their medications, and they let him go with no recommendations.

The hospital has sent him a bill for $700.00!

Talk about headaches! Does everybody get treated these ways? With the co-op members, it seems common. His question to me is, "Should I sue?" We'll research this one, too. For my part, it's good to be here, learning to be a neighbor, taking my part in the mix. Guide us, Lord.

## August 1999

Dear Friends and Relatives:

Ella Duffy went to Nicaragua July 23 to August 1. We are grateful to PATH (Presbyterian Answer to Hunger) for paying her expenses. She went with her daughter, Trici.

This report is in her words (with minor edits). (Ella will be one of the leaders of co-op #3.)

### Ella Visits Nicaragua

Leaving home for the first time to visit another country and not knowing what to expect was not easy, but this opportunity was welcomed. As I prepared to leave I prayed the Lord would take care of us. We all met at the airport at 6:00 a.m. to start this journey. I really didn't know any of the people that I would be traveling with other than my daughter Trici. But as we gathered together, I didn't meet a stranger; it was like extended family. We were on our way to Nicaragua.

Our arrival was great. We went to our hotel where we had lunch; we already had lunch on the airplane, but out of respect we ate again, then we took a shower and a nap. We just took it easy until suppertime when we had the pleasure of Rev. Norman Bent who talked about his work here in Nicaragua to try to make changes. After supper we all retired for the night.

Well, it's Saturday. We went to the Marie Elna Cuadra Center which housed the movement of employed and unemployed women. Our host was Esperanza Carderan. She told us about the battle women had to face to get employment even if they had been trained. After she finished talking, we returned to our tour of Nicaragua. A guest, Pat, joined us who was from Miami. The group she was with had been to Russia. We visited a lot more attractions and enjoyed every second.

There were the times we stopped at corners and children would ask for cordobas (money) and we could not give them any. Adults were on every corner selling things from water to bumper stickers and food; some had chairs and floor mats.

We arrived in Tipitapa where we visited for a while; the children were so friendly. One older boy tried to give my daughter his 7-year old son! There were a lot of children there; some were trying to catch fish for their supper. They had an old net which made their task very hard. We then went to our hotel to rest, have supper and get ready for the worship service in the morning. Sunday morning, we worshipped at the First Church of the Mennonite Fraternity; the members welcomed us as we arrived for the service. Although we didn't speak the language, we could feel the spirit of the Lord there. The scripture reading came from Mark 3:6-20. The speaker said always take time to meditate with God, not just on Sundays but every day. The service ended and the members thanked us for coming. We returned to our hotel for lunch. My knee was still giving me trouble—it was swollen more than ever. Thank God for great roommates—Ruth rubbed my knee with some tiger balm and put ice packs on it. *Thank you, Ruth.*

Well, it's finally Monday morning. We arrived at CEPAD, a ministry of evangelical churches working together in emergency relief and peacemaking throughout Nicaragua. We had orientation and went to the community of Casa Blanca, our home for the next five days. All the children came running to help us with our bags; these young people were overjoyed to receive us. We all visited with the families of the community; then we found out that the old school would be our living quarters—it had been washed out by Hurricane Mitch and our beds were mattresses on the floor! But that was ok with everyone. We had lunch and went on visiting and taking pictures with the different families. They like for you to take their picture. We had supper and went to bed early for the next day was a work day.

We got up early to work at the new community, *the new Casa Blanca,* to help put roofs on 21 houses. Everyone had a job to do. I helped to make concrete to build walls; some people put on roofs. The next few days were spent putting on roofs. By the end of the week, there had been five roofs put on. On Friday, all the children came and we had so much fun.

Then it was time to depart; we all said good-bye and went to the bus to leave. Oh, yes, there were tears shed by most of us.

Well, for me, this was the best 10 days of my life. I learned I can still live without hot water, telephones, air conditioning, curling irons and television. The outdoor bathrooms were a challenge, but we did survive and God was always with us. Thank you for this experience and I look forward to an opportunity to return.

October 1999

Dear Friends and Relatives:

Friday the 15th we began our third co-op! What a joy! Kenny and Ella are off and running. Seventeen new families who had gone through our orientation came and we had a great time. Mark and Ella brought lots of food for our new families. For snacks-on-the-spot we had cheesecakes and other too-rich foods from the Atlanta Community Food Bank. Ella took pictures of everyone and we put them on a new "Georgia Avenue Food Cooperative #3" bulletin board. Again, I must thank the Presbyterian Hunger Fund, which granted us $10,000 to begin this new co-op.

One of the households of Georgia Avenue Church is an intentional Christian community, which happens to be located in the house next door to where I live. Several of the community members had jobs at an Italian restaurant in a fancy mall in north Atlanta. Without warning, the restaurant managers announced one morning that they were closing the restaurant *that day*!

I got a call on a Monday morning, my day off, from the restaurant assistant manager, that they were closing and offering us all their food! Even on my day off I couldn't turn down an offer like that, so I headed off. We got pasta, meats, fish, cheese, biscotti, spices, mushrooms, cooking oil, juices, gelato, etc., etc., along with cutting boards, table cloths, pans—I don't remember what all. I made two trips, taking along my son John and some men from the church that were among those who lost jobs when the restaurant closed. That work was a lot of fun.

We loaded our freezers, but the food was not in the right quantities and form to hand out at our co-ops. After puzzling over it, we decided to have a party for the church, especially since fellowship time is in short supply these days. The members of the Christian community offered to be the cooks, and did they ever! We had loads of food, and still ended up taking a large box of thawed meats, which we knew we couldn't cook in time, to the Union Mission (where one of our other church members was working).

We had hardly gotten started when streams of people whom we had never seen started pouring in. I'll bet as many people came in from outside as came from the church. They were coming from the Task Force for the Homeless, which has its offices across the intersection from us. I'm pretty sure our friend K was the one who issued invitations. We fed a number of mothers with children—for a moment they had a feast, and the Lord used us to provide for them. That was a blessing.

On Sunday morning several of our church members spoke about how meaningful it was to them to share the time with and provide for those who were homeless. I must say, though, my emotions were mixed. It is wonderful to have the privilege of serving those in need. But in all honesty, I was tired, I was ready to stop, and I had looked forward to the meal as a time to fellowship together with other church members; a time to relax and visit, not another time to have people in need soliciting me to meet their requests. I did not end up enjoying the time that much, even though, as I say, the whole thing was a blessing.

There are places in the scriptures in which the Lord is reported to be tired, and yet he is set upon by crowds of people. He ministers to them and does not turn people away. So far, we are not turning people away. But right now, I do feel stretched.

One specific prayer that burdens me is that the Lord would make a way for Mark, my partner, to work here full time. I can see that he is tired, too. He raises his own money to work here part-time, just as I do, but raising enough to be full time is another story. So, we need resources from beyond us. Right now he is torn between two jobs; it would make his life so much easier, and we could be so much more effective as a community ministry, if he could work here full time.

The Lord is good and I am confident he will make a way for us. He has seen us this far, and as I always say, I am where I am supposed to be. As always, I continue with gratitude for you, for your thoughtfulness, your faithfulness and support, even though I never see most of you.

November, December 1999

Dear Friends and Relatives:

This letter is a greeting for Advent and the Christmas season to you who have supported me in a variety of ways. I tell you often that I am grateful, and I do so because you have sustained me here. I am very appreciative. Some of you have stuck with me a long time, trusting me and being faithful with your prayers and money. I am practically moved to tears as I think of the way the Lord has provided for me and my family through you.

We have fed many people. We have formed important and long-lasting relationships with our co-op members. People have stopped drinking, parents have started caring for their children in new ways, people's lives have been changed because of our work. Is it earth shattering? No. We do not make headlines. But we have been used of the Lord in a powerful way, and I firmly believe more is to come. I do believe that. I have said before and I still feel that our work, our co-ops in particular, are a slow-growing plant that is still just a tiny, tender shoot. More is to come.

Before long we will have 150+ families in our food co-ops. These families are families who are struggling, and coming together even on this small basis makes a difference to people's lives. I see wonderful, beautiful people who are absolutely of no account in our society, and it is a privilege to be able to minister among them, even in the limited ways in which I do.

Thank you so much. I wish I could visit with each of you individually, and perhaps that can happen someday.

For now, blessings on you in this Advent season and in the upcoming Christmastide.

January 2000

Dear Friends and Relatives:

The writer of this letter is Mike Armstrong, who along with his Christian community, is a member of our newest co-op. I asked him to share something about the way he experiences the co-ops, and these are his reflections. Thank you, Mike, for writing.

Can you remember a time when you were so young that you could play with a simple toy or even just your imagination for hours upon hour without a worry or care in the world? Could you say that you fully experienced that moment? Of course you could, your entire world was that moment with the toy or fantasy. Wouldn't it be wonderful if we could live that way now as "adults"? I feel as if the Lord wants us to experience all of life in that same way. Fully. Christ came "so that we may have life and have it to the full." With that perspective I have been able to experience so many more wonders and blessings from the Lord in my life.

Recently graduated from college, I was unfamiliar with life more fully and was faced with the many choices and challenges young adults face in the United States, the "What now?" dilemma. Fortunately, I knew the Lord and I knew that whatever I chose to do I would do for him and through his love. This meant serving people and so my choices were limited. However, I soon discovered the motivation behind my life choices was not from God. Being one who sought to serve through justice, I kept my eyes and ears peeled for chances to challenge injustice. I discovered so many injustices and evils in the world and in my city, Atlanta. I could fight these injustices and serve the Lord. But in my search to serve I missed life. All I could see were the rich getting richer, the poor getting poorer, the poor losing their homes, the homeless being jailed, the poor going hungry, and so on, and so on. All of this suffering and pain blinded me. Sure, it motivated me to fight for justice, but where was the joy? Where was life?

Only since the Lord began to teach me to be present have I known life fuller. This means being present in my mind, present in the lives of others, and present with him. Only since I gave up seeing only suffering, worrying about tomorrow, and removing myself from being ministered to, have I come to see that God is doing good; the poor are being fed, lives are being changed, brothers and sisters are being made, and life is being lived fuller right here in Atlanta, in little ol' Georgia Ave. Church.

I am a member of Georgia Ave. Church and also part of an intentional Christian community and we are members of Food Co-op #3. In addition to receiving food, I get a chance to be filled by the Lord on a bi-weekly basis. On every other Friday at the co-op the Lord chooses to appear in many different ways. Whether it's in the smiles of two older women laughing over shared experiences, a four-year-old girl nicknamed "Woobby" running around the food tables, or in a conversation with Ella Duffy, one of the co-op coordinators, Christ is always present there. Moreover, the work of Christ is just as present every Wednesday at the lunches that are served. Being part of an intentional Christian community frees me up to be a part of the Wednesday lunches also. Women and men, many of whom are homeless, have the opportunity to sit around a table together and eat and hear the words of Fay Romero and Pastor Chad. As food nourishes those who eat on Wednesdays the life of Christ is given the chance to flourish through the conversations across the tables, the ministry of Fay and those like her, and through the diligent heart-pouring work of Mark Jordan.

What a blessing Wednesdays and Fridays have been for me. Each week I am reminded that God is good. The lives of Chad, Mark, Ella, Kenny, and the ministry that they are can remind us all that life is fuller and that just as Christ remains present in our lives and with Georgia Ave. Community Ministry, we must remain present in order to live this life we're given to the fullest, joy and pain together. Thanks be to God for giving us the ability to experience joy as well as suffering. Without it, I don't know how I'd be able to be that child again, being fully in the moment, smiling at life.

Mike Armstrong


February 2000

Dear Friends and Relatives:

Our third co-op is going well. We have added more members, so that at the moment there are thirty families, and we are about to add up to ten more. Our goal is a total of fifty families (brought in gradually, so that everyone can get used to the changes, get to know each other and adjust). The total number of families in all three co-ops is 120 presently.

In October, I mentioned to you the need for Mark to be able to work full time here, both for his sake and for our ministry. I appreciate that several of you responded with concern and even, in some cases, money toward that end. The Advisory Board which is working with the community ministry has made a plan to have in place by the fall an endowment that would ensure Mark's salary for three years, starting in January, 2001. The goal is to have pledges and/or funds of around $75,000. I will be updating you on this periodically. We've got a long way to go, but already we are encouraged by the response.

A member of our church, Lou, is the nurse at a Christian-based non-profit health center that has its space just across the street from the church building. Recently, she shared in our church service about a woman who came in there and was telling her how important the food co-ops are to her. This co-op member did not know that Lou was a member of the church. This woman has severe respiratory problems and battles depression; she can do very little without getting worn out. But she told Lou that she so much looked forward to being at the co-op meetings; that those meetings are the highlights of her month. Hearing that kind of thing can carry me a long way; it gives me the energy to keep working.

As you know very well, we do not have a lot of money, but for our people just being connected to the church and the community ministry gives people something of a lifeline. I think of that because two people have been calling me in the last few days; we connected today. One of them cannot pay her rent and needs $40 to help her make it; another needs $271.00 to keep her gas on. We can't pay the whole gas bill, but we said we could give her $50 toward the bill, with a letter that she could take to others. Sometimes if an agency or church sees that there is someone else helping, they will chip in. This woman has already gotten the gas company's assurance that if she gets them *something*, they will not cut her gas off. She is a woman who is not well and has *no income* at the moment. How she makes it at all is beyond me. Our benevolence account is in the hole, which is quite often the case, but there are requests that I, we, just can't turn down. Very often, in the Lord's hands, our little bit becomes enough; the Lord takes our concern and the concrete effort/money we put toward meeting the need and makes it work, at least for one more day.

With the church's blessing, I am going to take a bit of a break starting in March. I will take the month of March off completely, and will continue to be off the next three months from the church while returning to work with the community ministry. I would be ever so grateful for your prayers during this time.

## May 2000

Dear Friends and Relatives:

I'm back up to my old tricks. Can't get my newsletter out on time :-(.

This last Thursday, I spent a few minutes with the members of Co-op #2 asking the question "What else could we do together that we are not doing now?" Our co-ops are so good: people get food they wouldn't have, people get to know others they wouldn't know, people get support they wouldn't have, people have their faith strengthened when they otherwise would not—much happens. But it is small, and each co-op is actually together only once every other week (though we see many of the people between meetings).

Anyway, I brought the question. At first, not much happened. I eventually said, "Would a credit union be of any benefit?" Oh, yes, oh yes, was the response. On a scale of 1 to 10, the reaction probably got up to a "4." Then a young woman said, "I would like to see us do some things for the children..." and she talked a little about that. Not a huge response—maybe a 2 on that one.

Then Jackie began to talk about her dream that we could start a restaurant down on Georgia Avenue near the stadium. It would be the "Georgia Avenue Co-op

Restaurant": "I know how to cook chicken... and look at all the people we could put to work—our ladies could be greeters out on the street, Melvin knows lots of people he could bring in...!" People got to moving in their seats, there were some amens, and interruptions, and the power just began to pour from that room. "We could have something of our own—I wouldn't have to go off to that little job across town where they pay me just $6.00 an hour –not enough to live on! I'd be right here. And we'd make some money for the co-ops...." She went on and on. I was on fire myself hearing her talk. This wasn't coming from Chad—it was coming from the co-op members themselves. On the 1-to-10-reaction scale, it was about a 20! This was dream being spoken, of poor people having something of their own, something they had a stake in. I could feel the longing in Jackie, and everybody else was swept along.

And then it was time to end the meeting. I left, but the power of that moment stayed with me. I took Jackie home with her food box and we kept talking. She talked about how the co-op had helped to sustain her and her 3 children when she was at a low spot, how when she first started, people would laugh at her and others walking their carts of food home! And now, those same folks have all joined the food co-op!! She spoke of the struggle of being poor and black in this society, and a woman with three children to raise by herself in a tough neighborhood, and how her oldest son had just delivered such a moving eulogy at his grandfather's funeral. She was so proud: "I didn't know he had it in him." It's always a test for mothers here— "how will my children turn out when everything is against them?"

It is hard for me to hear all these longings. Living at the intersection of two worlds presents its own pains and dilemmas. I hear longings such as these about the restaurant being voiced—but have I stirred that longing up for nothing, just rattled the cage yet am nowhere near having a door opened through which she and others can walk to realize that dream? I am both moved and frustrated—"How long, O Lord, how long?! Will you make a way? You who own the cattle on a thousand hills, can you provide for more than just sustenance for us? Must we be stuck in the mud making bricks and never fly?"

I choose to believe that these dreams are related to future reality, that we would not have the dreams if our God were not bringing them about. Something about these kinds of dreams is like being "psychic"—we **are** seeing the future; it is being born in us. Our God heard the cries and groans of the Hebrew slaves, so we know God hears our cry. We are longing and crying. Hear our prayer, O Lord. Come to our assistance; make haste to help us. Forge from these yearnings the stuff that is yet to be; do a new thing and mold from this deep suffering the building blocks of what we do not yet see but hope will be.

### June 2000

Dear Friends and Relatives:

This particular spell was a bad one. Constance was holding his hand; she said, "It's all right, Big Hawk. I'm with you. You can relax." He did, and he passed on. Feels like the end of an era. Constance, who as you may recall is mentally challenged, was an angel in Hawk's life. Years ago, she kept after me to go with her to visit him in jail, the result of which he became a Christian. So she's the one who has aided her father to let go of his old lives and midwifed him into the new. We buried him yesterday; he was 69. He had had a series of seizures that left him in a coma and landed him in Grady Hospital; he struggled to get breath and hold on. I'll miss him.

My last letter reported Jackie's dream (Jackie Palmer, the coordinator of co-op #2) as expressed in one of our co-op meetings. I said just maybe we are seeing the future. It makes my heart sing to think of people having dreams that might actually come about, dreams of self-expression, of having a living wage, of having a sense of respect about themselves, of having a desire to make a contribution to the community. Jackie's dream contains all those elements. Such a dream comes from deep suffering and longing, years of waiting and being overlooked and stepped on.

There has been a response. The first thing that happened was that the PATH Committee (Presbyterian Answer to Hunger), which has been looking for new direction, decided upon hearing about Jackie's dream that that desire is exactly the kind of thing PATH needs to be backing. The committee has decided to do just that. It is not yet clear all of what that means, but Sarah, the director, has already begun to join in discussions at our church building. Sarah and PATH bring a wealth of information and contacts, and a certain legitimacy, especially with the overall Presbyterian Church, that we do not already have.

Second, two other people have come forward with other dreams: a dream of a coffee shop (by a Georgia Avenue Church member), and a dream of a co-op store (by a church member who is also a member of the co-op).

Third, the doctor who operates the non-profit Christian health clinic across from the church, and I got to talking. He has been working for nearly two years to get land on which to build a new clinic; he already has money to build. But he has been blocked thus far. We ended up being led to propose that the restaurant/coffee shop/co-op store people begin to work with the doctor to see if together we can get the land we need and get these businesses off the ground. That proposal has been accepted.

So, we have begun to have meetings together about bringing into being a place in which all of us have space and work together, and we came up with the name "Georgia Avenue Coming Together." We are co-op members from Summerhill (the combined years these 3 women have in Summerhill is well over 100); poor, not poor, super-educated and under-educated, new and old Summerhill residents, black and white. We want to keep the old residents from being pushed out; we want to incorporate some of the new people who have moved in; our co-op members want to make a contribution toward forming the new that is coming and not just let greed and developers' money call all the shots; we want to provide living wage jobs for some of our people; above all, we want the Lord to be glorified, and we believe that such a demonstration of the lion and lamb lying down together will do that.

We know that this dream is impossible. Only God

can make it happen. On the one hand, it is laughable: a group of nobodies meeting to form businesses and place them on land that is coveted by many—many who have money and influence. But that's our dream and we believe it's come from the Spirit. So we're ready to "dream the impossible dream" and work toward it. Pray for us.

### July 2000

Dear Friends and Relatives:

A lovely elderly lady, Louise, is a member of Georgia Avenue Church. Since our service is informal and there is time for people to share their concerns, she sometimes shares her needs and praises, and it's not unusual for her to want to sing for us, just to "thank the Lord." It's always touching for me when she does that, knowing how difficult her life is.

One of her daughters is in jail—drugs. These drugs ravage the community. How does anyone in poverty resist their lure: the money, the status, the escape to a new reality at least for a moment? They take lives, separate children from their parents, husbands from wives, etc. Louise has several children, most of who are doing well, but this one is not. This leaves Louise to take care of the two children of the jailed daughter. They are 2 and 3 years old; Louise is 72. It's a lot for her. Still, she comes and she sings and it is heartfelt.

Louise's 55-year-old son was her favorite. He used to take his mother fishing every week, and when she had a car, as she does again now, he kept it running. They talked on the phone weekly, sometimes at length. He had back pain and the doctor decided an operation would be the remedy. He came out of the surgery paralyzed from the waist down. For a while, she was taking care of him, too, in her apartment.

We buried him last week, dead after being paralyzed for 15 months. He left six children who he seems to have cared for, the youngest being 13-year-old twins.

Did he get the best care? Is this one more black man who didn't count quite enough so that it was easier to slip up? I don't know, but these kinds of accidents seem to happen more often to those who are the least in our society. So Louise has buried her son and is deprived of his strength, help and support. Louise is tired and sometimes gets depressed, but when she is able, she will still come to church and sing to the Lord.

Betty is a co-op member who is raising her great nieces. Same story, except in this case it is her niece on drugs and in jail! Betty has severe back pain herself. Her doctor, too, wants to do surgery, but she is afraid to allow it. We pray with her, and I referred her to a chiropractor whom I see and who was helpful to me with my herniated disc. Everything's not perfect, but she believes that slowly he is helping her. I pray the Lord will bless her, because I know she is in pain. I am grateful to the chiropractor, who is treating her at no charge.

Monday, I had the privilege of aiding one of our church families to move into their first home. I've written about this family before: he was a teen-age gunman who spent 26 years in prison, they lost twin infants, he has bladder cancer: they've been through a *lot*. They have been living in an Atlanta Housing Authority project, in an apartment that has a terrible problem with mildew, which the apartment managers can't/won't fix. The couple was, of course, worried about how this was affecting them and their children. Beyond belief, they qualified to buy a home.

They were *determined* that I was to pray and bless the house *before* they moved in, but on Sunday, when they were to "take possession," it was unclear whether in fact they would get the keys, so after the church service we decided to put it off until we were certain. Well, they called Sunday evening; they had gotten the keys and "could we go ahead right then?" To be honest, I wasn't jumping up and down to go out at that point, but I said "sure" and a few of us were able to go with them to their new place. What a blessing! I'm glad I went. The new owners were overwhelmed and rejoicing, as you can imagine—they have a yard that's fenced, a screened porch, a bedroom for both of the boys and themselves; this little house is like a castle to them! It was a wonderful moment to share. We walked from room to room, praying and giving thanks. It is quite clear to them and all of us that the Lord has acted, because on paper, this whole thing looks impossible.

Finally, I want to recognize my oldest sister, Barbara Ann. She died last week at age 53. She had MS for the better part of a decade, and had gotten to the place where she could not move, could not eat regular food, and could barely talk. She was a sweetie, though, and cheerful to the end. I would ask you to keep my mother in prayer, and Barbara Ann's husband who was devoted and faithful through it all.


### August, September 2000

Dear Friends and Relatives:

This coming month will be an unusual one for us. Our church has orchestrated, through members and friends, the means for us to make a trip to Greece for a whole month!! It is related to the sabbatical-type break I took in the spring and to the fact that we are about at our 20th year anniversary being here. I am so grateful to our church and friends. Barbara's father was of Greek heritage and Barbara identifies very much with that heritage, so it is also with that in mind that the church made its gift. I'm not sure how they pulled all this off—a family of 4 for a month; our church is not that big. It's a miracle!

Since I will be away much of September, I will ask you to indulge me by letting this letter suffice for both August and September.

I received a call from a professor at Emory's Candler School of Theology. He wanted to know if I would meet with him and another professor from Candler regarding assigning students to work with us during the fall semester. I was glad to do so. The class is an ethics class and the professors want to put students in situations where values clashes are happening in the life of the city. In our case, it's how we work to address the situation of people in neighborhoods experiencing gentrification that threatens to drive them out. (There was an article in last week's *Atlanta Journal* touting how much "better" Summerhill is since the

Olympics; however, the perspective from "the other side" is quite different. In a recent meeting, Martha Baynes—who is an elderly co-op #2 member, part of our "Georgia Avenue Coming Together" effort, a 33-year resident here and so cute—said, "Ever since the Olympics, Summerhill has been going down.")

I asked the Candler professors if they would present their request to the members of Co-op "#1, who were meeting that day. One of the professors was able to stay long enough to do so, but then had to leave once questions were clarified. We continued the conversation in her absence and the co-op members decided having the students with us would be a good idea. But Mark and I also needed help deciding where to put these people "to work," as that is part of the assignment. At first, people said, "Sure, they can fill boxes." I said, "Wait a minute! We're not going to have them doing *our* work. This is *our* co-op and our work to do. We've got to find something else." Mark thinks well about these things, and came up with the thought that we could assign the eight students to spend their 12 work hours doing research regarding resources which might be available to us. The idea struck everyone as inspired; now we need to figure out the particulars.

Just about a month ago now, Fay was given as an anonymous gift of a new car (1986? station wagon). It looked good and was clean; she was so tickled to get it, as her old car was such a ragged junk heap. She hadn't had it a few days when it was stolen. She didn't hear anything about it for more than a week, and finally got a call that it was at an impound lot. She went over to get it and when she saw it she just cried: it was totally stripped and torn up and of no use to anyone. Her son has an automobile, and is making a way for her to use it during the day while he is at work. But that cannot last. If any of you have a car that is still useful that you might want to donate to her through the church, please let me know or contact Mark at the church.

I have many prayer requests: Pray for Mark and our staff in my absence. Pray for Kenny, co-leader of co-op #3, who is having some problems with his hip replacement and has had to be in the hospital. Pray for me and my family on this trip. I am not an experienced traveler! And finally, pray for provision for the community ministry, as I seem to be struggling with grant proposal writing and, anyway, can't write proposals while in Greece.


October 2000

Dear Friends and Relatives:

We are back and so thankful for the gift of being able to travel to Greece—such a gift. Here's a brief report.

We arrived Sept. 12th, John quite motion sick, all of us worn out from a 10-hour all-night plane ride. Our taxi driver didn't speak any English and we didn't know where we were going to be staying, so we were immersed immediately in the trials and adventures of travel in a foreign country.

Barbara, with Helen's help, did a fine job with our translating. Barbara had us packed just right, too—we didn't have too much but we had what we needed. We each had a backpack, a water bottle, and one "stewardess" size rolling suitcase, into which we managed to get everything for a month, and room for gifts coming home! We were apparently an interesting sight as we walked along the streets, often in single file; if there was a sidewalk, it was 18" wide in places. We went from place to place without having any reservations when we arrived. In fact, after we left Sparta, we went south and took our only ferry, which was to Crete. We were told the ferry would leave at 5 (though we were also told 4). We got to the ticket office, where they told us 7; the ferry left sometime after 9. We arrived in Crete in the total dark at 4:00 a.m., walked with our luggage down the pier in this little town not knowing how to get to the village to which we were headed or where we would stay, and we sat down at the outdoor tables of a little taverna and used a flashlight to read the book *Cheaper by The Dozen*, which we had brought for entertainment. Through strange circumstances, the Lord provided a cab around 6:00, so off we went, and found a wonderful domatia overlooking the beautiful deep blue Mediterranean Sea.

Highlights include, for me especially, going to Mars Hill and the Agora in Athens, and being able to "walk where Paul walked." But it was also such a joy to go to the villages in the mountains (these mountains are something; I had no idea) to see the places where Barbara's grandparents had grown up. We did not know if there were relatives or not. We took a taxi from Sparta, and went into the mountains to the town center of Georgitsi (yor-yeet´-tsi). There were some people sitting at an outdoor table. We began introductions, and lo and behold, one of them was Barbara's cousin! She showed him the family tree that she had with her and it turned out that his brother was the one who had compiled it. We then went back down the mountain to the next village, and found relatives there, too. The Lord had worked out the timing perfectly, as we had not even planned to go to those villages so soon in our trip. And, finally, Santorini was definitely a highlight –so dramatic and beautiful. Santorini's beauty is the result of a cataclysmic volcano that is supposedly the most powerful of which we have any knowledge (@1450 BC). Our rooms were on the caldera wall facing out across the crater.

We ran into problems with transportation and other services. While we were there, the post office went on strike, government banks went on strike, service stations went on strike, the taxis went on strike, two ferries sank and inter-island ferry service (which we depended on) was canceled for 20 days, and then, at the end, we couldn't get on the plane with our buddy passes to get out of Athens! We ended up buying regular tickets to go to Rome where there were more flights available.

For all of us, it was the experience of a lifetime. We thank you and we thank the Lord. We never thought it would happen.

I end on a more somber note. While we were away, one of our most faithful co-op members, the president of our #1 co-op, Willie Mae Williams, died. This was unexpected— she was a young-and-active 66, but she had had trouble with asthma. She had an asthma attack, and fell in the night and hit her head. By the time she was discovered, she had passed. Willie Mae was also one of our regular shoppers and we depended on her. She wasn't always the easiest to get along with; as they put it at her funeral, "Willie Mae had her ways." She contributed much for nearly 10 years (including roasting a goat for every Summerhill reunion). We will miss her.

December 2000

Dear Friends and Relatives:

I look forward to this New Year with anticipation. We are nearly at full capacity in our food co-ops now, with right at 150 families. All three co-ops have elected steering committees which meet monthly to assess how things are going. Our newest co-op, #3, is just over a year old, and it is doing beautifully. With the prospect of Mark coming on full time in the spring, still other possibilities unfold. We expect to start a fourth co-op, probably by the summer or early fall, and by the end of 2002 we should have 200 families. This coming year we will begin to hold meetings to spread the word about our co-op model. The Atlanta Community Food Bank folks have already indicated they will consult with us on it. We have funds to pay our own co-op coordinators to do this work. Furthermore, thanks to the work of some of the Candler Theology School students, we now have our video equipment (a 27" TV, and VCR, on a cart, with money left for purchasing/renting videos—money from a $1000 grant) which can begin to be used for education, training and entertainment.

This coming year we will incorporate our effort to form small businesses, Georgia Avenue Coming Together, into a 501(c)3 organization. (We are already working on this.) By the grace of God, we will also find a location and actually form a restaurant, a grocery store and a coffee shop. The truth is, this is daunting, since at this point, we don't know much about forming such businesses—but I know it's right. Every time I hear Jackie talk about it, I am renewed in my certainty that what we are doing is good, and the Lord will make a way.

There is so much wonderful activity around our food co-ops, sometime it is just a joy to be there. Last Friday, co-op #3 held a potluck Christmas meal with their meeting. I had to leave and miss the meal to go to a meeting, and boy, I hated to go. The atmosphere was so alive with the joy of dividing up all the good food we had gotten at the food bank and the farmers' market, and the added fun of knowing a meal was being readied by some of the members; it was quite infectious. That is a joy for me that goes deep; there is a rich quality to such moments.

I've said often, our goal is that our members will use their gifts to extend and form this organization. They are doing it. I envision the day that I will work myself out of a job, and that someone in our co-ops will take over. My, that is a thought! I don't know how long it will take, and at times I have some fear and trepidation about it. (It's hard to think of losing control!) But I am certain such a direction is of God, and that God is even now raising up the right persons.

My description of the Georgia Avenue Community Ministry is always that of a slow-growing plant, coming up at just the right pace. Our ministry has already born fruit in people's lives: in people being renewed in their faith, people freed from alcoholism, individual's lives becoming more stable, people having others to lean on and call on, not just being "out there" so alone, people being fed physically, emotionally and spiritually. Joy comes in, relationships grow, even income and new work have come from our ministry. At this point, my sense is that the plant is becoming sturdy, and on the verge of bearing much more fruit than in the past. This plant is about to move to a new phase.

Many of you have been here all along, supportive in many ways, nurturing this plant in your own way. It takes patience; it takes endurance, longsuffering—characteristics that sometime seem in short supply in our fast food, fast-paced world. Thank you for sticking with me and us for so long. Your perseverance is reaping rewards. May our God bless you richly at this Christmas season.

January 2001

Dear Friends and Relatives:

I was sick with a pretty good case of flu last week. I'm grateful to be recovering, though still find myself weak. Unfortunately, it's the rest of the family's turn now.

Mark tallied figures on how much food we brought into our co-ops in 2000 to find that we had distributed approximately 170,000 lb., 48,000 of which was fresh produce. At the end of the year, we got all of our co-ops up to capacity, which means there were about 50 members in each co-op. I'll guess we averaged during the year 130 families (since co-op #3 was growing during the year), so that the average per family would have been something over 1300 lb. of food. Of course, larger families got more, smaller families less, but we averaged about 327 lb. per person with each family's program fees being only $52.00 annually.

Last Friday morning Mark, Ella (one of the coordinators of co-op #3) and I had a meeting with Rob Johnson, Carol Richberg, and Kathy Palumbo of the Atlanta Community Food Bank. They initiated the meeting, but brought a larger agenda than we expected. They have been working as part of a "collaborative" of various social agencies (health, housing, social services—I don't know what all) focused around homelessness and funded by Fulton County. Of course, if people are to maintain life in a home, one of the needs is food. The collaborative has begun to form food co-ops, based on our model. This piece has fallen into the food bank's hands, and Carol has been overseeing it. But she can't continue—it's too much for her with her other job responsibilities. So our meeting was to explore whether we would become part of the collaborative and take on the responsibility of consulting with the co-op that's already formed as well as starting a new one.

Unfortunately, the county doesn't want to provide much money for this, so whether we are really wise to get into it is questionable. It appears as though we will be expected to do a lot for a little. However, the food bank staff does need relief from doing this, and perhaps there will be unexpected opportunities in it. With a lot of uncertainty we are saying "yes," especially since Ella says she would like to work with forming the new co-op. It's an honor to be asked; if it's funded, we'll give it our best for a year and see where we go from there.

Spanga Gwabeni, one of our church members, who is a co-op member as well, works in a childcare center now. She would like to work in our community ministry, but we do not have enough work to employ her full-time. If any of you in the Atlanta area know of a part-time job with decent wages, would you please contact me? Because of an ongoing eye problem, she is not well suited to clerical work, and is dependent upon public transportation. She is a sharp and dependable person and I have no hesitancy recommending her to you.

As always, I continue with appreciation for your ongoing support.

February, March 2001

Dear Friends and Relatives:

We have been plagued in the last few weeks with more violent death among our young men here. Willie Mae's (our former co-op #1 president) grandson was shot and killed. He was only 15, but he was in the middle of robbing someone. Two young men from our local Southside High School were recently killed. One of them was a quiet young man who was a good student and liked by his classmates. The story I have was that he was shot 19 times; turned out to be a case of "mistaken identity"—the ones who shot him thought they were shooting someone else. The third young man was also well-liked, but like Willie Mae's grandson, he had begun to obtain things in an illegal manner, and at 19 is dead from gunshots while robbing someone. These deaths are hard: the last two were classmates of Fay's daughter, Christina, and about to graduate.

At least three, maybe more, of our co-op members live in an apartment building several blocks from the church. The building has just been sold apparently. Lucille (of co-op #3 and a former co-op #1 president) showed us the letter she received from the new management: her rent should be mailed *before* the first day of the month; it is late on the 3rd and the charge will be $155.00; on the 5th of the month the owners will begin eviction proceedings! Lucille's SSI check doesn't even arrive until the 3rd, and she has no checking account, so must send money orders. The owners know very well that that is true for many. I don't know what kinds of problems they have had had collecting rent, but I do know that Lucille, at least, is very punctual about paying her rent and is not one to complain about the lousy apartments and maintenance. (We had to call the previous owners who were failing to repair Lucille's heater in the middle of our coldest weather.) I don't know whether these requirements are legal, which I will work to find out. It may be that the owners are trying to push people out. It may be, too, that if we can talk with them in person, they will turn out to be better folks than they appear so far in print.

I wish so badly we could buy those apartments. There are three buildings; I'm not sure how many apartments, but a good number of people would be displaced and probably have to leave Summerhill if they were to be torn down. In my dreams, I see our co-op people living in and running them; but in reality, there is no money for buying them, no expertise about managing apartments and I don't know that they would be sold. If some of you have thoughts or would like to think with us about how something like this could happen in Summerhill, please contact me. The Lord works in all sorts of ways, and I don't know how many of you who read this have expertise and/or money for such a venture, but it would be great to find ways to put some brakes on the gentrification process and bless our people.

One of our newest Wednesday lunch attendees, who has also begun to attend church, needs your prayers. She has already had one foot removed because of diabetes. Her 19-year-old son does a wonderful job of taking care of her, but they live in a drug-infested boarding house. Many of her things have been stolen there; people have broken into her room and gotten their food and the TV, among other things. She told us in church that she really wanted to move out, but then returned to say that she felt convicted to stay to minister to those who are in the house. Right at the moment, she is in Grady Hospital and has just had the little toe and part of the other foot removed; the doctors had already determined that they would almost certainly have to remove one more toe, though they are hoping not to have to take the whole foot. She has been praying that she would not lose the whole foot, as that would make it much harder to get around, and harder for her son. We've been praying for her. I visited with her Friday and prayed with her. I just talked with her and she is so excited: the doctors found that they do not need to remove another toe after all, and her foot looks better than they expected, so she has a reprieve for now. The Lord has answered our prayers. She is an amazing new addition to our body; her attitude is wonderful (the nurses at Grady all love her). Pray for her strength and wisdom and "soul force" in the house in which she lives, and for physical healing.

This letter will serve for February and March, as I am once again behind. I continue to thank God for your continued support. May this Lent/Easter season bring new life to you.

April 2001

Dear Friends and Relatives:

Recently I asked you to pray for a woman with diabetes and foot infections. She did end up having to have that foot removed. She is still struggling with infections, and her doctors are now advising her to have more of her leg removed. She most definitely needs your continued prayer support.

I have a nice mental picture of her, which I want to share: one day before this most recent operation, she came to the church building needing food. I gave her all we had. It was near the end of the day and as I was heading out of the building, I thought I could hear voices outside. When I went out, she was in the street in her electric wheelchair, dividing her food with a man who was also in a wheelchair. She hollered to me saying he, too, had come for food and she had enough to share; her face was radiant with a wonderful beatific smile. While I watched, they turned and started down the street, a black man in a red wheelchair, a white woman in a black wheelchair. It was touching to watch these who have to struggle against so much smiling and talking as they rolled off.

Two Fridays back, some co-op members plus a few other interested parties walked, singing, from the church building to the lots on Georgia Avenue on which we are praying/planning to plant our little businesses. We wrote to the Atlanta Development Authority in February inquiring about the availability of the land, but we have not had the courtesy of a reply. So, we are appealing to a Higher Authority. Taking a cue from Joshua, we went to the land and marched around, singing and praying; we asked the Lord to bring the "walls" down—walls of money, politics, influence, etc. We are only one of several parties interested in that land, and the least influential. It is a moving thing to hear our folks sing and pray out there in the sun. The only thing we've got going for us is our belief that the Lord is in this, which gives us inspiration and determination. It is absurd for us to be expecting to build on, rent, or own that land; but in our society, being part of something absurd is often one of the few sane options. So much of the scriptures are about absurd acts in which little, unknown nobodies are used of God to accomplish great things. Several folks have said, "But you don't have any money!" That doesn't bother us; being small and nobody and having no money is a plus in this business.

We were contacted by the small church committee of the Presbytery of Greater Atlanta and informed that Georgia Avenue Church had been chosen the "small church of the year" for the presbytery. I thought that was rather broadminded of them, given that we are not actually a full-fledged Presbyterian church. The minister who called me to inform me of this said that much of the acknowledgement is related to the way the church reaches out through our community ministry and the food co-ops.

It is not my intent to write a letter every other month; I just get behind. So, this letter is for April and May, which is why I'm including two envelopes for those of you who contribute regularly. I am so appreciative of the ongoing support which many of you provide. I am very blessed to be here, and I owe much of that to your trust and generosity.


June 2001

Dear Friends and Relatives:

Our neighbor across from the side of the church had her car stolen a few weeks ago. She stopped Mark and was quite upset with him and let him know that she was going to circulate a petition in the neighborhood to force us to stop our programs. Mark relayed her frustrations to me. We have to take her seriously, since she has said such things before. But I did not rush over to see her, hoping she would cool off a little.

A few days later I bought some flowers and went to her door. The Lord had preceded me. She welcomed me and began to apologize about her behavior. She said the Lord had convicted her that she had not been right in her actions or attitudes. She was happy to receive the flowers and we talked and prayed together. She has since gotten her car back. I also invited her to have lunch with our co-op #2 members a few days ago; she joined them and had a delightful time.

I am grateful to the Lord for working in this situation. We definitely don't need escalating animosity with our neighbors. I do not think our people are the ones responsible for these acts. In fact, just two weeks ago, as we were holding an evening class in our church, K, an alcoholic who prides himself on being our "security," came bursting in to tell us that he had seen someone throw a rock through Art's (church member) truck window. K had run and hidden. I asked him who it was, and he said it was nobody he had seen around the church. I was relieved to hear that.

The Georgia Avenue Coming Together effort at forming a grocery store and a restaurant is still moving along, ever so slowly. We've had the most difficult time finding out who owns the land on which we wish to build. Months ago we wrote to the Atlanta Development Authority, whom we are told is the owner, but they have not given us any reply. However, Ella found out that decisions about what will happen with the land rest with a local community development organization.

We decided that several of us would go talk with the director to see what it would take to buy, rent or build on the land. Four of us agreed to go: Spanga Gwabeni, a church member and member of co-op #1; Martha Baynes, who's lived here forever and is a member of co-op #2; Ella Duffy, coordinator of co-op #3; and I. We met in my office ahead of time to pray and talk about how to approach the conversation. We agreed that I, the only white person and only man in the group, would *not* be the main spokesperson, but rather that Ella would, since this effort is a co-op members' initiative.

We went to the director's office and sat down together. He came in, and began to direct all of his talk to me. It was "Rev" or "Chad" this and that, (I am quite informal about titles), and even though he is African-American like my colleagues, he did not speak to them, only to me. I kept quiet. Martha got increasingly impatient as he kept talking and eventually said loudly, "Ella, don't you want to say something!?" Ella kept biding her time, and finally Martha said even louder, "Ella wants to say something!" (It was so funny.)

The upshot of the conversation is clearly that, while we were not told "no," we are not in favor. "Summerhill needs a 'major grocery store' and not some 'mom and pop' operation." And while "the community can express its opinion about how this land is to be used," we left knowing that this man can and will throw roadblocks in our path. He never asked us anything about what we have planned.

We're not discouraged. We know more than we did, and we know the battle is the Lord's. We visited Pharaoh and he doesn't want to budge. So, what else is new? We've heard that story before. Do keep us in your prayers, for though we know the ending of that exodus story, we are in the middle of this one.

July 2001

Dear Friends and Relatives:

As I begin this letter, it is my birthday. I am very grateful that I have had as many years as I have; I know they are not something one can take for granted.

My youngest child, John Luther, is 13. He loves playing baseball and is quite good at it. It is such a joy for Barbara and me to see him play and be with him in that. This last week his team won the Pony League state championship for 13-year olds. John was the pitcher in the championship game; I was more nervous than he. He enjoys it and he thinks well on the field. It's a delight to see my young ones doing well (also not to be taken for granted!).

Winning the state championship propels us to the next level, which is a regional tournament. We (the families of the players) have been raising money to make this trip to Round Rock, Texas. All of a sudden, we were thrown into practically forming a little business to raise $13,000 plus within about a week for all of us to make this trip. We have succeeded, and will leave tomorrow (Friday, the 20th) evening on a tour bus.

All of that is great, but I am aware that I live in continual culture shock. So many of my families in the church, and certainly in the co-ops, struggle so to make ends meet. I met with the parents of one of our church member families yesterday morning; they work hard, getting up in the night, having to leave their children at odd hours for their job. They never make enough money. Right now, the wife has a toothache from a wisdom tooth that was never pulled as a youth, but no insurance to pay for it and no "extra" money. Recently, I noticed that their front tires were showing wire through the treads. They couldn't afford new tires; I spoke to a local tire storeowner, who gave them new ones at no cost, for which I am most grateful. But that is only the tip of the iceberg; their car insurance is expiring and they haven't money to pay for it. The church is able to cover it, but, again, there is more. This is just one family among many. I'm not talking about lazy bums; I am talking about Christians who are poor and who have struggled for so long. It takes a toll on them. They grow in faith, yes, but they work and see no light at the end of the tunnel. Meanwhile, a group of us can raise $13,000 for a one-week trip to Texas for baseball! Sometime it's hard to hold these worlds together and it raises questions for which I have no answers.

Acts 2 presents the picture of a powerful and caring church, in which no one was in need, and people sold possessions to make sure all had enough. In that kind of church, it was easy to evangelize, because others could "see" Jesus in that loving generosity. I don't see that today. What keeps the church from being that kind of community now? We have a good and caring church at Georgia Avenue, and though none of us is rich, there is much generosity among us; even so, the emergency charity that characterizes us seems to fall short. And in the church generally, those who are better off often make a point of staying away from those who are poor, separating themselves for safety and comfort. So, "the poor" become a distinct and isolated class.

In my recollection of the teachings of the Jewish Talmud, the highest form of charity is to provide jobs for the poor in such a way they do not know who has provided; the second highest is to provide jobs such that the recipients know the source; the third highest is to give money to someone in such a way that they do not know their benefactor; and the lowest is to give money in a way that the recipients know who is giving. All of that is well and good, but even in that prescription, "the poor" are a category set apart from *me*. It seems to me that there is a higher level of care for the poor, and that is to join our lives with their lives so that we are together, not separated, and it is no longer "the poor" but "us." That's what Jesus did; he came to be with us in our poverty. In our community ministry, the Georgia Avenue Coming Together effort to form businesses is not to form businesses "for" the poor. Rather, "they" are "us" and "we" are working on forming the businesses *together*.[5]

---

[5] We did, in fact, finally form a self-development business, a restaurant named Tummy & Soul. Ella came up with the name. Alas, like many restaurants, ours lasted about 2 years, (roughly between 2002 and 2004), because, among other things, the area

Still, in the church, I pray for the Holy Spirit to break down these have/have not barriers even more. It cannot come by legislation. I do know that for me, being less-than-comfortable myself and having a church community and ministry in which many are poor economically by US standards, pushes me. Even so, I am grateful to the Lord on this 56th birthday that I can be in this place. Come, Holy Spirit.


## August 2001

Dear Friends and Relatives:

Gas deregulation in Georgia has hit our people hard. It has shifted a lot of costs to poor people that they did not have before. Martha Baynes, one of our co-op members, is one of them. She is elderly and has had a lot of health problems. She had an arrangement with her new gas provider to pay $75.00/mo., but the company called her to inform her that they were planning to cut her gas off the next day, because they said her bill was over $2000.00!

Martha came by the church that day and was telling me about it; she said her blood pressure had never been higher. "But," she said, "there is nothing I can do but put it in the Lord's hands." There is no way she could pay it; she only receives $386 a month. We were complaining together, and laughing, too. She is such a cute character: funny and feisty, with a great laugh. Well, somehow, Martha was interviewed on channel 5 TV regarding high gas bills. I missed it! When she came to the co-op Thursday, I asked her about it, and she was so tickled. She said a judge had called her and told her he had seen her and was going to send her $100, plus they were going to take up a collection in his office. _Then,_ Martha was interviewed on NPR's "Morning Edition," August 23, in a story about high gas bills in Georgia! I couldn't believe it! After that a woman from Tulsa, OK, called Martha and paid her gas bill in full!! The Lord certainly worked in a "mysterious way" to answer

---

around us did not blossom as predicted. The inevitable gentrification came, but not soon enough for Tummy & Soul.

Martha's prayer, as $2000 was nowhere in sight when we prayed together Friday. And the bill was not just paid; there will be additional money in her account. (The NPR website lists their programs and you can listen to that interview—it's worth it.)

Jackie, one of our co-op #2 coordinators, said gas employees have been going up and down her street putting locks on gas meters. She said the *Atlanta Journal* reports that companies are working overtime to cut off 2500 homes every day, five days a week. They had been cutting them off 4 days a week, but couldn't keep up at that rate. It's going to be interesting when winter comes. In the NPR piece, one company spokesman called people who are delinquent "deadbeats," but Martha was paying them monthly as arranged.

In the most recent issue of *The Other Side* magazine there was an article by a woman named Judy Anne Eichstedt, who had been homeless. She says, "I have slept in cars, under bridges, in homeless shelters, and in abandoned buildings. I know what it's like to be on the streets with my husband and our six children. I also know how it feels to be homeless and alone.

"Our family spent almost five years going back and forth from poor and barely making it to homeless and living on the streets. We spent several months living out of our worn-down battered car, traveling not only from city to city but from state to state trying to find work and a place to belong. We learned to expect the odd looks from people who would see us sleeping in a rest area when we were too tired to go on. But when people would laugh at us (as if there is something funny about being homeless), it cut deep into our hearts....

"When my husband would return in the evening with news that he hadn't found work, it was hard to hang on to hope—let alone have faith that tomorrow might be a bit better. When a potential employer hears that you have no home address or phone, you're shown the door quickly. Going to a job interview in clothes you've slept in gives you little chance. People assume that anyone who is homeless is a drunk, an addict or guilty of some crime. There's nothing you can do to change their minds.

"Sometimes my husband would stand by the road with a sign that said 'Will work for food.' If I could, I would join him, since people tended to be more compassionate when a woman was standing there, too. Still, people would drive by and yell horrible names at us, throw their drinks on us, or shout 'Get off the streets!' A few times, people spit right in our faces...." (July & Aug., 2001, p.27).

Judy Anne is a Christian and now lives in her own home, a Habitat for Humanity house, with her children. For many of us, it's easier to deal with folks like her and Martha if we write them off as "deadbeats" or call them names. But when we hear their voices, then our hearts are touched, and we remember that we are neighbors.

The scriptures admonish that we must be mindful of those in need: "Those who despise their neighbors are sinners, but happy are those who are kind to the poor." (Proverbs 14:21) and In Luke's gospel, Jesus says, "Blessed are the poor, for theirs is the kingdom of God...." (6:20).

An important part of what moves me has to do with responding to people who are poor. Just speaking economically, the number of people who are poor in our country is considered by the Economic Policy Institute (EPI) to be about 80 million, or 30% of the population. The Congressional Budget Office (CBO) and the EPI, say that the government-set poverty income line should be about $36,000 for a family of four (at the time of this letter the official government poverty guideline was $17,650)! The CBO reports that between 1979 and 1997 the average after-tax income of the bottom 20% of our population went *down* $100 to $10,800, while the top 1% went up $414,200 to $677,900 (*The Washington Spectator*, Aug.1, 2001, p. 2). Presently, the minimum wage is $5.15/hr., which works out to $10,712 before taxes; at $5.15 that salary would have to be raised $2 to restore the minimum wage to slightly less buying power than it had in the late '60s. (p. 2).

September 2001

Dear Friends and Relatives:

Bobby, one of our co-op members (who helped me write this letter), was arrested in the spring for selling drugs, which he swore to us he had not done. He had sold drugs in the past, and he had been honest with us about that; so we believed him when he said he was innocent this time. Though it looked as if he was selling drugs, he was not; he was selling other items on the street. He's a good salesman, peddling perfumes, oils, clothing items, etc. However, he had no vendor's license and the police knew he had sold drugs in the past, so he was arrested and spent nearly five *months* in jail awaiting his trial, unable to pay his bail.

The public defenders did not get anywhere with Bobby's case, so Mark and I called on the Georgia Justice Project. Doug Ammar heads the program; he used to be a member of the church and we know him well. After some research into the matter, Doug took on the case. Georgia Justice has an excellent program that includes putting clients to work in their landscaping business and hooking them up with drug rehab programs. Mark and I went to court (again!) to speak for Bobby at his hearing in the hope that, based on the program that the Justice Project had worked out for him, the bail would be revoked or the case might be thrown out altogether. We and the co-op members had been praying for him because, even though he had a bad record, we were convinced Bobby was on a new track and was innocent of the present charge. But the judge was not sympathetic; he reduced the bail, but it was still too high to pay. Bobby was dejected, but with help from us and others, we did get Bobby out to await his trial.

Two weeks ago, Bobby appeared in court for a judgment, and at this Thursday's co-op meeting, he told us what happened. He said he was sitting before the judge awaiting his decision, facing *thirty years to life* given his past record! So when he stood in front of that judge, the same one who had been unwilling to revoke the bail, he knew it was a decisive moment. He placed himself in God's hands. The judge asked him if he had anything to say. Bobby said,

"I'm asking you to have mercy on me and the people that have been supporting me. I am going to finish my course" (complete the program Georgia Justice laid out for him). Meanwhile, the DA had been reading Bobby's record out loud in order to sway the judge toward a tough line.

The judge sat there and then started shaking his head, saying, "It's by the grace of God; it's by the grace of God... I'm sentencing you to 3 years' probation and to finish the six-month program Georgia Justice has laid out. God is with you today!" Bobby said other people in the courtroom couldn't believe it. When he walked out, some people told him they, too, had been praying for him to be free to continue on his new path.

There's more: before Bobby was arrested, he had gotten a ticket for not having proof of auto insurance, but the court date was set while he was still in jail. Of course, Bobby couldn't appear at court. So, after the drug verdict, he had to appear at traffic court the next day. Bobby brought his insurance papers, but the judge basically said "too bad," and fined him for "failure to appear in court" even though he was in jail at the time!! Bobby said, "I can't pay; I have no money." So the judge said, "Then I sentence you to 40 hours of community service." But after they left the courtroom, the judge came out looking for them, and said, "I'm going to suspend this sentence. I don't know why I'm doing this. You're just beating the system... you're just beating the system."

Bobby knew why the judge(s) was (were) doing this—God had acted. The One who created the universe stood by this lowly "nobody," and answered his and our prayers. It was wonderful to hear Bobby tell about it at the co-op, and thank God, and us, for praying.

I am ever so thankful to Doug Ammar and the Georgia Justice Project, to the co-ops for supporting each other and praying, and to you for your continued encouragement.

On a much different note, my family needs a car in the worst way. Our car, which was itself a gift a couple of years ago, for which we are very thankful, is needing a lot of costly repairs, for which we have no money (and our mechanic says we shouldn't put the money into it). If you're in a situation in which you or someone you know might have a decent car that doesn't need a lot of work, which could be donated to the church for our use, it would be a great help. It would be best if it were automatic, because of my wife's back problems that the constant shifting of gears aggravates.


December 2001

Dear Friends and Relatives:

I wish all of you could sit with me in some of our co-op meetings. They can be so powerful. When people gather who have so little by modern US economic standards and give profuse thanks and praise God for all the *many blessings* that God has showered on them, it is profoundly moving.

This last Wednesday, one of our church attendees, about whom I wrote briefly on a previous occasion, finally got up the nerve to sing a song she had written and composed. Teri has had both legs removed, she has irritable bowel syndrome and a type of neuropathy that is steadily shutting down her muscle and nerve functions. She is a sight, sitting in her wheelchair, playing this small keyboard with one hand and holding a microphone in the other. She had told me she writes lyrics and composes music, but I didn't give a lot of credence to that, since I hear some version of that regularly and seldom see evidence of any creativity. But to see this crippled person performing, and hear her singing so well a song of praise to God, was such a beautiful gift. I am very blessed to be in a situation where I can receive such gifts, and not only at Christmas, but all year round.

Having potlucks has grown steadily this year among our co-op members. Of course, this Christmas season is a good excuse for eating together. There was a potluck meal today for co-op #2, and Tuesday there was one for co-op #1. Since yesterday was Wednesday, and the good people at Second Ponce Baptist served our Wednesday meal, that's three days this week we were feasting at the church building. I have to say, it is joyful.

I so much yearn for that day when we will all sit

together at the Great Banquet Feast that our Lord is even now preparing. I do not handle well the strain and suffering of the present age; the dislocations of the time are for me sources of great grief. I wish the Lord would not tarry. Festive moments such as this season point us to that day when

> They will not hurt or destroy
>     on all my holy mountain;
> for the earth will be full of the
>     knowledge of the Lord
> as the waters cover the sea. (Is. 11:9, NRSV)

But we are not there yet. Advent is a good season for me, for "come, Lord Jesus, come quickly" falls from my lips regularly. It is the season of that yearning.

Meanwhile, we wait. A German pastor of the last 19th century, Johann Christoph Blumhardt said, "... [A] lazy waiting [for Christ's return] ...is not appropriate, for the life of the faithful is itself the beginning of the end, and upon the faithfulness of these forerunners everything depends...." (*Thy Kingdom Come, A Blumhardt Reader*, ed. by Vernard Eller, p. 42)

May the Lord bless you in this coming Christmas and holiday season and in the coming new year. May we wait faithfully.


March 2002

Dear Friends and Relatives:

It was a pauper's burial, paid for with city funds: funerals are often a struggle in our community. I picked up Fay and drove to the funeral home for the services for Pat Riggins, one of our co-op #2 members, knowing that other co-op members would meet us there. The service was right here in Summerhill; Fay and I were the only white people in attendance. It was so good to see how well our co-ops were represented at the service: Jackie, Fay's co-op #2 coordinator-partner, was on the program to speak, and it was listed in the program that Pat was a member of the food co-op. Two other co-op #2 members were listed as well, Mrs. Fannie Bradley, who prayed, and Christine Shivers, who sang; when the funeral director realized I was present, I was asked to read a scripture. There was a real sense to me that the co-ops have won a place in the community over these eleven years, and they give our members a bit of standing. The preacher did well, and pointed out Pat's work in the co-ops toward feeding people. (She was a quiet but faithful worker.) Most importantly, the service was a fitting celebration of this poor woman's life.

It was good, too, to learn more from others about Pat; I didn't know her much apart from the co-ops. A younger woman was there who was a crack addict. She testified that Pat had never turned her away from her door, and that when she was at her worst and had to be in jail, Pat had taken her children and raised them. (Pat had no children of her own and was not married.) She did a lot in ways that few would recognize.

A group of us from the co-ops (Jackie, Fay, Ella, Ella's daughter, Trici, and I) had all piled into the co-op truck and driven up to Sandy Springs in north Atlanta to visit Pat in a hospice there. She was hardly recognizable, cancer had wasted her so. The women ministered to her so beautifully. Some of them had spent years around Pat and knew her in ways I did not. It was touching to be there, to witness their care, and to have some part in ministering to her. She knew we were there and she said little things from time to time to let us know that she was hearing us. She died a few days after our visit. A staff member at the hospice stopped us as we were leaving to get information from us about her funeral plans, etc., because they thought we were family, as no one else had been around. It turns out there were family members, but they do not live here in town, and so were not in good touch with the hospice staff. That visit was not the only time members of our co-ops had visited with her during this illness, but I am glad we visited her when we did; she knew she was remembered and loved. Our co-ops fill a much larger role than putting food on people's tables, as important as that is.

We are in the midst of changing our Friday food co-ops to Tuesdays. We have been finding we are not getting as good foods on Fridays. The change will cause some adjustments, but should be good in the long run. In any case, for those of you who might wish to visit, please note the change. You are as welcome as always; we'd love to have any of you visit at any time.

We do find ourselves stretched financially, so please keep us in prayer. We need money for food and for salaries for our coordinators; it would be a blessing to be able to pay off our truck on which we still owe about $10,000. Some of you have been so helpful toward keeping us going; I am very grateful to you for your prayers and encouragement, and in some cases, financial contributions. Pray for me and our newly elected Board of Directors as we approach foundations, etc. Isaiah 43:19 reads, "The Lord makes a way in the wilderness...." Jesus has been faithful to make a way for us, and in this Easter season, I am more confident than ever that will continue.

May 2002

Dear Friends and Relatives:

I have obtained a copy of Jackie's son's book, *Signs of Love, Signs of Pain*. It is rap poetry about being a young black man—some of it is kind of raw, much of it touching and revealing. It is pretty real and honest. The "book" is really hardly more than a pamphlet and is $7.95. Marwan's (pronounced Muh-wan') experience is much different from that of most middle-class people—many of his friends have been killed, many others are serving terms in prison, but he has gone to college and has turned in other directions. Jackie has done a marvelous job holding onto and raising her kids by herself, and at least in small degree, our co-ops have helped her do that. I don't recommend the booklet if you are easily offended, but if you want to hear the voice of someone growing up in a family in our co-ops, you will find it worthwhile.

Jackie's daughter is a pretty girl who will soon turn 19. She has a job; she worked hard to get a car that will get her to her work. Over the weekend, she pulled into a gas station down the street from us, and two guys pulled up behind her, jumped out of their car and demanded the vehicle. She backed off as quickly as she could hoping they would not force her to get in and would not hurt her. They didn't. Her purse was still in the car, too; so far nothing has been recovered. When Jackie told us about the incident, we spent time together lamenting, but also praising God and thanking him that her daughter hadn't been abducted or hurt.

Today we held our last Wednesday lunch meeting until September. The truth is, I hate to end those meetings. We are able to form something of a community with the folks who come on Wednesdays during the school year— especially with those who come not only to eat but also to participate in our prayer and worship service. We host children's programs in the summer and don't have the space to do both. So much needs to be done, but we can't do it all.

Especially for those who come to the service, it can be a rich time. On our good days, besides going away filled physically, people feel cared for and honored, maybe even filled spiritually. One woman who came today had a scar across her neck: someone had jumped out at her with a knife this weekend. She was doing pretty well, considering; the wound had not ended up being very severe. She was new to me; we spent time praying with her. Another couple asked for prayer about finding housing. I talked to the man during the meal, and learned they have to be out in two days and they have found nothing yet! She clearly has some sort of mental problems, so they don't want to move too far from Grady Hospital, where she receives care, but the truth is, housing prices are going up so much here, people are being pushed farther from Grady. But he was hopeful; he said the last time they had needed housing, they had had us pray for them and walked out of our service and right into a place.

A couple of weeks ago, J, a gentleman in his 50s who has mental problems, was crying, *wailing* out loud. Fay and I sat with him over the meal as he reminisced about his long-dead mother and about not having a family. A handsome family came in late with about four children—I didn't get to talk with them as I was needing to leave, but fortunately we still had food. Were they homeless? S was going to bring her son with her today; she wanted him to talk with me, as he is getting into trouble in school. She didn't show. It is a momentary community of vast need, but the gathering brings with it hope and momentary respite. It's a blessed time.

But the summer will be good, too. Using the space to minister to children is something that will bring dividends to their young lives. Ours is a building well used, well used for the purposes of the Lord of Life. Keep us and our people in prayer.

June 2002

Dear Friends and Relatives:

Diane is one of the presidents of co-op #1 (the steering committee decided to elect 2 instead of pres. and v-p). She has had so much with which to cope. Her son has mental difficulties and she has his children living at her home; her own health problems have been growing; her mother lives with her. Her mother has Alzheimer's disease and is increasingly more difficult to manage and is not eating right. Diane also has taken into her household a young woman who is deaf who has no other home. They are all stuffed into a rather small house and more are coming.

At the last co-op meeting, Diane stopped me to tell me this story. She said she had gone to the grocery store to buy food for the children and "Ensure" for her mother, which is about all her mother can keep down. But she did not have enough money for the food and Ensure, too, and began to cry in the store. When she was telling this to Mark that morning at our co-op meeting, one of our shoppers, Victor, heard her, ducked out and came back in a few seconds with a bag full of Ensure! One of our other members had brought it from the place where she works. It was a wonderful co-op moment and illustrated so beautifully how bringing people together in the name of the Lord can make a difference to their lives, to their ability to keep on keeping on, to their faith, etc. Diane was certain that the Lord had acted on her behalf.

I checked the messages on our church phone late last week to hear a call from a neighbor woman, J, who seemed to make a point of not giving her last name. She wanted to know why there is so much activity around our building and whether we are staying within the bounds of what we are zoned to do. I assumed we are, but I decided to do a check on the issue: yes, we're within our zoning rights. I tried to call J back but only got a machine; she has not returned my call. It sometimes feels like there aren't too many folks in our neighborhood who reach out to their neighbor-in-need. The Task Force for the Homeless has moved; the Family Store and the Grant Park Health Clinic have moved. Our ministry to our neighbors in need, who are fewer and fewer in Grant Park proper but very close to us, in Summerhill, Peoplestown, etc.—we're talking walking distance here—no longer fits the agenda of gentrifying Grant Park, so it gives us a marvelous opportunity to witness to the Jesus who identified himself with those who were hungry, in prison, etc., and in need. We strive to be faithful not only to "Jesus-in-the-sky" but to Jesus our neighbor on the earth. It is a blessing to be blamed for too much activity at a church building, especially since I suspect strongly there wouldn't be an issue if most of those involved were white and middle-class.

I went with Ella, one of our co-op coordinators, to lunch recently to visit and assess how things are going for her. She told me something I had not known before. When she first came to the co-ops, she had terrible trouble with her legs because she had what was diagnosed as osteoarthritis in both knees. Some days she couldn't get out of bed without rolling onto the floor and was in constant pain. She spent most of her time lying or sitting because it was so painful to move, and the condition was progressing. She was depressed and hurting and did not want to face the days. But all of that had changed for her. Maybe we're doing something right!

I was flabbergasted. I didn't know Ella that well and wasn't around her much when she first came into co-op #2. She will readily admit that when she first came she just wanted a box of food, to do as little as necessary and wanted meetings to end as soon as possible. But the Ella I know I really began to know only a little while before she entered our leadership class when Mark and I were looking for leaders to form and lead co-op #3. We chose her/God raised her up to be one of the leaders and Ella is energy personified. She is a great coordinator. She is "take charge" in a good way, and from my perspective, a very good candidate to take over the job of being the overall co-op coordinator when the time is right. I would never have guessed she had had such physical limitations.

So I asked her what had happened. She said being in the co-ops had brought healing. She didn't know exactly what had happened— she has been drawn back to the Lord and she just knows that now she has purpose and has this ministry and she wants to make it succeed and she isn't plagued by the same physical problems she used to have. The pain is not all gone, but it is much less and she doesn't let it stop her—she can get up and be on the go and has life now that she didn't have. Now instead of getting worse she is getting better.

You can imagine these stories keep me going. These testimonies verify to me the value of forming community and bringing people together in the name of the Lord. Ella knows she is feeding families; Ella knows she is making a difference to people's lives. She has received healing and the Lord has used the co-ops as an instrument of newness for her. Diane can see how she is being sustained by what is provided her and has support she gets nowhere else. (Both Ella and Diane gave permission to pass these stories on to you.)

Please recognize that your prayers, your financial support, your concern and energy are part of what our Lord uses to make our mission possible. I know that I could not be here without your help, and I know that I can say without boasting that my role has been used of God to help form this work and keep it going. That is a joyful gift and as always, I continue in thankfulness.

July 2002

Dear Friends and Relatives:

I really like the theme song we have adopted in co-op #1. The chorus is

> *Let it be real, Lord,*
> *Let it be real.*
> *Let it be real, Lord,*
> *Let it be real.*
> *Everything I do for the Master,*
> *Let it be real.*

The verses follow along: when we work, Lord..., when we serve, Lord..., when we pray, Lord, let it be real. We can add any verse, of course, and for our co-ops we added the work and serve ones for ourselves. It's a simple enough song, as you can see, but is itself "real," with a simple and melodic tune. One of our members led us in singing it one day and it has become our song. We hope that what we are doing is not fake or insincere, and that song is a prayer itself, that God will honor this desire.

I am excited to refer you to our fledgling website at "gacm.org". Mr. Larry Jenkins (a member at Second Ponce de Leon Baptist) and Mr. David Lower (a member at Central Presbyterian) of our board are putting this together. I'm most grateful for their work. The site is "under construction," but it is a start and has a couple of pictures. The "gacm" is for Georgia Avenue Community Ministry, of which the food co-ops are the largest single program. If you have the means and get a chance, check it out.

Recently I wrote to you about Jackie (coordinator, co-op #2) and her son, Enorris Marwan, the young man who published a small book of poetry. She was sharing with me yesterday her joy that she had gone to his graduation at Ft. Valley State College and what a celebration it was. Marwan graduated as Salutatorian of the class; his picture is a main feature of a large poster that greets people coming into the school. She said there were 5000 people at the graduation and many members of her family had been able to gather and rejoice with her. Marwan has been given a scholarship to pursue a masters degree in economics at Georgia State University. I am so proud of him and of her; my gosh, that woman has fought against so much to have her children turn out well. You cannot imagine! (Just two months ago, we were expecting Jackie at a meeting. When she was with us at the church earlier that day, she had said she would be present. We learned later that she had had to run home because two of Marwan's cousins, brothers who are his age, had run to Jackie's house after killing another young man because of arguments about drug money! She urged them to turn themselves in; one of them ran, the one who claimed he was not the triggerman turned himself in. I'm serious when I say there's been a lot to fight against!)

I turned 57 in July and I am aware that the Lord has been so kind to me all this time. And many of you, as well, have been supportive for a long time. I am grateful.

# Section 3

# Remember Jesus!

Our ministry has had a long association with several local churches whose pastors and certain members have supported our efforts in a multitude of ways, including regularly being on site with our people. Because of this, not only have the relationships between our organizations grown over time, relationships have developed between those church members, most of whom are comfortable financially, and our folks. I think everyone involved would say that these interactions have brought new perspectives and additional richness to their lives.

I have often been asked to speak about our work in Sunday School classes and worship services; however, when the conversation leads people beyond their current comfort zones—especially conversation about material wealth and crossing social classes—it can be particularly challenging. I was asked to teach a Sunday morning adult class for a month at an affluent church. I prayed about it and felt led to do so, and then had to pray about what I would teach. I was given liberty to go where I understood the Sprit to be leading. For me, what usually comes from my heart and experience is to teach and preach about the place of the subject of poverty in the scriptures and the life and teaching of Jesus.

Coming from a world where the average income of my co-op members is less than $12,000 annually, I was literally coming to them from another world. I worked on what to teach and felt at peace about it.

At the first meeting there were close to twenty-five people. Given the room size, the place was pretty full. I told them what I had in mind, I told them some about my world, I read three or four of my newsletters and then I talked about the importance of the theme of poverty in the scriptures, about how our Lord was himself poor and that his first recorded sermon beyond, "Repent for the Kingdom of God is at hand," was "I have come to bring good news to the poor...." I said that our Lord himself was supported by women who followed him and the disciples around. Someone in the class raised a hand to ask in what sounded like a bit of a challenge, "Where is that in the scriptures?" (Luke 8:3) It seemed to be new information to him. I didn't feel antagonistic or any need to beat people over the head; I just wanted to lift up the importance of this theme, partly because in our society poor people are forever being battered, treated as though they are worth less because they have less, and I thought it important to clarify to my church brothers and sisters that such a stance isn't one we as Christians can adopt, that people who are poor are important to the Lord who was himself poor and identifies with those who are.

When I came back the next week there were just seven people. The person who had asked me to teach had called me ahead to warn that there *might* be fewer people the next Sunday. She said that one woman had said to her, "Those newsletters were so *sad*!"

This is a church that puts a priority on being faithful to the scriptures, so it made sense to teach from the scriptures, but for one reason or another only a few in the class were choosing to hear what I had to say on that particular subject. I told them that I would not be offended if they did not want me to return, but they wanted me to come back. None of the others returned, but the remnant, including the man who raised the question about Jesus being supported by women, came back every week. It was a significant step for them toward engaging this rather charged issue.

I do not believe the importance of the subject of poverty in the scriptures can be overstated; it is essential to study and to hear at all times, but it seems especially important in our present atmosphere in the US, even though it's an inconvenient theme that raises uncomfortable questions, and runs counter to the secular American dream and values. It is not the primary stance of the scriptures, as I understand them, that people who "have" should be *helping* poor people; it is that in the church we are to be a new family of every class and race loving one another, as Jesus said, "...as I have loved you." We are to learn from each other and look out for each other as members together in the new family of God. The One who is the Head of the church calls us to be together, "working out our salvation with fear and trembling" (Philip. 2:12). Those who are not in need are not to seal themselves off in comfortable, "safe" church settings. If we do so, we put ourselves at risk, as was the case for the rich man in the following parable.

> 'There was a rich man who was dressed in purple and fine linen and who feasted sumptuously every day. And at his gate lay a poor man named Lazarus, covered with sores, who longed to satisfy his hunger with what fell from the rich man's table; even the dogs would come and lick his sores. The poor man died and was carried away by the angels to be with Abraham. The rich man also died and was buried. In Hades, where he was being tormented, he looked up and saw Abraham far away with Lazarus by his side. He called out, "Father Abraham, have mercy on me, and send Lazarus to dip the tip of his finger in water and cool my tongue; for I am in agony in these flames." But Abraham said, "Child, remember that during your lifetime you received your good things, and Lazarus in like manner evil things; but now he is comforted here, and you are in agony. Besides all this, between you and us a great chasm has been fixed, so that those who might want to pass from here to you cannot do so, and no one can cross from there to us." He said, "Then, father, I beg you to send him to my father's house—for I have five brothers—that he may warn them, so that they will not also come into this place of torment." Abraham replied, "They have Moses and the prophets; they should listen to them." He said, "No, father Abraham; but if someone goes to them from the dead, they will repent." He said to him, "If they do not listen to Moses and the prophets, neither will they be convinced even if someone rises from the dead."' Luke 16:19-31 (NRSV)

This parable is one that I find remarkably relevant to the mainstream church now. I referenced it several times over the years in the letters. If I place myself within the story, I would be the rich man. I am not actually financially rich by US standards, but relative to my co-op members and people in poverty in the world, I am a rich man. When one of our co-op members came to my rather modest home to see me, her little children came in marveling, saying, "Is this a mansion?" By the grace of God, I have been enabled to actually sit at table with Lazarus, embodied by Constance and others in our church, the homeless people who populate our Wednesday meal times and members of our food co-ops. What a great blessing it has been.

In the parable I think Jesus has placed himself as Lazarus, Lazarus who actually *does* come back from the dead to summon us. Lazarus means "God helps," "Jesus" means "God saves." Who is God saving in the story? Me! The Rich Man. God is endeavoring to rescue the rich man, who, as we know, was on his way to Hades, a place of torment in the afterlife as the parable characterizes it. God is also endeavoring to provide for the poor man who was in need in the here and now. We know our Lord is concerned about people who are struggling materially. And our Lord is just as concerned about people who are *not* struggling materially, the ones who can be stuck holding on to the "heaven" and "security" they've already got (Matthew 19:23-24) and miss the deeper riches they would otherwise gain. The story tells us that Jesus' remedy for the needs of each was fellowship, relationship, removing the gated fence and meeting together over a meal at the table. It turns out that in God's economy we're to be together because we *actually need each other*. Get rid of that chasm and we will find life!

An important point not to be overlooked is that the rich man is not consciously being greedy and selfish, as people typically conclude. He is instead being a good churchman, being "holy," setting himself apart. The assumption is that the rich man is a man favored of God. Why? Because he is rich! He eats well and is dressed well and is an elder in the synagogue, a deacon or trustee in the church. He cannot touch Lazarus, who is obviously *not* blessed, because Lazarus is a sinner. Why is Lazarus assumed to be a sinner? Because he is poor and hungry and sick with open sores! If the rich man touches Lazarus, his brother in the faith, he will become ritually unclean, and then he will have to undergo the humiliation of the required rituals to become clean again, and his reputation and standing will plummet. His dilemma is not that he cannot materially afford to help Lazarus; it is that maintaining his status does not allow him to relate to Lazarus as a brother.

According to Jesus, the rich man is setting himself apart in precisely the wrong way—keeping himself apart from the very people that Jesus embraced. Jesus did not tell us to "...love the Lord your God with all your heart, and with all your soul and with all your mind...and *keep yourself pure*." He said, "...love the Lord your God...and love your neighbor as yourself," i.e., make sure your neighbor has what you yourself need, even if it means risk, the risk of becoming unholy or even sick or unclean! We are to be set apart as people who do the will of Jesus, not people who are looking out for ourselves.

In the parable Jesus highlights an even deeper concern than that of individual failing, and that is a dynamic that the religion of the day was set up to collude with this "keep yourself pure" posture, set up to bless and encourage the *suppression* of compassion for another. The religious establishment was agreed that that was what Jesus' "Abba" wanted, but, of course, Jesus did not agree. The authorities concurred that it was the will of God, and banded together to keep themselves from those who might inconvenience or scare or somehow threaten them, from those who are somehow "less" than we, from those who are not "blessed" as we are and need what we've got. We don't even want to think that we might get so free in Jesus and so concerned for our neighbor that we up and sell our beachfront home (or whatever), as Barnabas did in Acts 4, to make sure everyone in the church can eat and pay their rent and get the medical help they need. If we set ourselves apart from such folks, we can't know them "up close," we won't feel their hurts or know their needs, and won't have to be worried about them. But this is the opposite of what Jesus calls us to and is a stance the parable tells us does not lead to a good place, because if we don't want to be at the table with such folks here and now, we can't be at the table with them then and there.

Another way of looking at my own journey over these years is that I have been schooled in the "prosperity gospel." These stories are about becoming wealthy! I, the rich man, have gotten rich in a *whole different way* being at the table with Lazarus. The Lord has had mercy on me.

Do I have money in the bank? No. Do I have stocks and bonds? No. Do I own a lot of property? No. So how am I prosperous? I am prosperous with life and love. I have shared life with beautiful people and have listened to and lived through amazing stories; I do not need to turn on TV shows to have adventures; I have learned much about caring and faith and depending on God from those whose lives are under tremendous strain; and from their ways of coping and enduring I have learned more about appreciating life. I am much richer in love and in relationships; I feel good about the work I have done and the setting in which I have lived; I am being taught to love my neighbors, whoever they are, as myself, and have learned that I am not God. I have become much more of a human being.

Moreover, I have had the joy of being able to contribute something in return. I have pastored a very economically and racially diverse group, from folks like Constance who were illiterate to those with doctoral degrees, from feminists to fundamentalists of many denominational stripes, all working together to forge a community that many have reported has had lasting effect on their lives. Our food co-ops have provided food and, in most cases, food security, which freed the members from huge stress and worry, and freed money for them to pay their rent or mortgages (and not become homeless). Some members have become leaders, and within our program have even obtained small jobs, jobs that pay a living wage, which has made an important difference in their income. New community has been formed through the co-ops so that folks have support they didn't previously have, working together and aiding each other. In many cases co-op members have been enabled to give to others, reporting that they even have enough food to share with their neighbors. I have the blessing of knowing that my life has been used to make a genuine difference to many people. I have given a little and I have received much.

I pray everyone who reads this book is or will become "rich" and prosper greatly. I hope you will not need to be forgiven your daily bread, because you open your hearts to the compassion that wells up from within your soul. Really, by not being willing to open our hearts to our "sadness" we close ourselves off to life. So, the secret to getting rich is to embrace Lazarus and invite him to your table.

How does one do this as an individual Christian? Generally speaking, with exceptions, of course, I don't think we do. I'm not advocating autonomous heroics. I came to this area with our little house church, which as a body was seeking a deeper relationship with God through deeper relationships with neighbors trapped in poverty. I'm suggesting you pray and address the matter in your church. Find likeminded brothers and sisters, those who might be looking for more, for deeper life in Christ. Pray together and seek ways to call your whole church to become prosperous in the ways of Jesus.

Many churches and pastors have a theology that invites their people to become economically prosperous; this dispatch is a summons to the church to become spiritually prosperous in a different way than that which reading the scriptures and studying and praying with your own kinds of folks will afford. My appeal to the comfortable church is to become earnestly intentional about developing prosperity, to mine the diamonds and other rare jewels that are hidden below the surface of the sorting systems of our society. Seek the ways to enter into life with those who are of different races and classes and nationalities, and do so *respectfully* without assuming you know how to "shape them up." "Lazarus" may not come to Sunday morning worship times. No problem. Find other ways. If you as a people seek, you will find. It may take a while, but pray and persist. The Spirit will guide you.

I'm not suggesting that what I am urging you to do

will be easy. It wasn't for the rich man; it wasn't for me, as you know if you've read the letters. But it is rewarding; it's definitely rewarding. I do want to reiterate, though, that I'm not advocating charity at a distance; I am talking about *being with people, developing relationships*. By actually relating to and getting to know and love people who are not like us, we can become wealthier and healthier spiritually than we can just about any other way. In my case, I'd say it turned me upside down and forced me to seek God at deeper levels than I knew I needed to.

The picture reflected in the scriptures is one of economic diversity in the new church, of Lazarus and the rich man being together, of walls being broken down, of a church in which there were Christians who were not secure financially. And that made for struggles, just as it does for us in the twenty-first century. In the book of James, as the early church grappled with these issues, the church was warned not to play favorites with those who were better off economically (James 2:1-9). 1 Corinthians 11:17-22 relates Paul's harsh admonishment to the Corinthian church because of those who were humiliating brothers and sisters who had less. These are but two examples of those in the church who were struggling with relating to and caring for each other across class lines. The subsequent verses in Corinthians teach that we are to share the bread and wine in remembrance of Jesus so that we are not creating such divisions but "discerning the body," taking into account the whole, not just ourselves, and caring for one another, working toward loving unity. It was a struggle but they were *together* working at it, clearly not always immediately successfully, given that they, like us, had imported into the church the socially stratifying values of the culture. But we're to be a new community, a beloved community, shaped by the values of Jesus. There is no doubt that to do so is difficult, but the battle is important; it is a central piece in the ways the Lord renews us and transforms our minds and conforms us to the image of Christ, forming new individuals and a new society.

Even now it is widespread in the church that we are stratified and isolated in our homogeneous groups; therefore, *it is our work to pray and put in the effort to create the conditions where we have to engage the struggle* instead of disregarding Jesus and only worshipping with and relating to those with whom we are comfortable. How can we share in the Eucharist, communion, the Lord's Supper, "in remembrance" of Christ (1 Cor. 11:24) if we are not embracing the poor but subtly or otherwise making sure they are not at the table? (Matt. 25:31-40; Luke 14:13-14). Remembering Jesus is not just a mental exercise about how we think; it is a social exercise about how we relate to one another and whom we include. We're in a moment where to "remember" means, to some degree, "re-member"— intentionally embrace new and *different* people, those who may not be able to put so much into the offering plate. If we are unwilling to do so, we have to ask ourselves whether we are actually choosing to *forget* Jesus, the Jesus that when walking among us was *poor* and identified with "the least."

So, this is an invitation to you and to your church: remember Jesus and move toward true prosperity, prosperity in which we all have what we need both in this life and the next.

# Appendix

## Covenant of Call and Vision of Georgia Avenue Church

### To Seek and to Know God

Those of us gathered as the body of Georgia Avenue Church are here because of our desire, individually and corporately, to seek God. As recipients of the redeeming grace of God in Jesus Christ, we want to know and to glorify God and to be a people of prayer. In response to God's grace and love in our lives, we are committed to taking seriously the needs of our brothers and sisters, and endeavor to love our neighbors as ourselves, both within our church and beyond. In doing so, we believe we will discover Jesus Christ in more real and meaningful ways.

### To Develop Community

We hope and pray that the Holy Spirit will bind us together as we learn to value, identify with, encourage, accept, listen to, support, and love one another. In our life together we desire to be characterized by joy, compassion, celebration, creativity, honesty, service, hospitality, generosity, spirituality, commitment, and faithfulness. Essential for the health and growth of such a community is the recognition and use of the Spirit-given gifts and talents that each person possesses. We commit ourselves to calling forth, welcoming, and nurturing these gifts, for the strength and enrichment of the individual and the community.

### To Be a Community of Hospitality

Although Christ through the cross destroyed the barriers that separated humanity from God and people from each other, our world still creates divisions based on race, money, education, gender, age, nationalism, and religion. We, however, envision being a church community which breaks down and bridges the barriers of our larger society and thus lives out of the deeper reality of what Christ has accomplished. To create a community that includes persons from all backgrounds and walks of life, we commit ourselves to be a people of hospitality, exhibiting a spirit of welcome to the stranger, regardless of his or her strengths or weaknesses, inviting all who would to join us on our journey with Christ.

## To Be a People of Hope and Healing

Our prayer is that we be a people of hope and healing for ourselves and for all who come among us. We realize that if this is to be so, we must accept and embrace both the joys and sorrows of life. We must keep before us at all times a keen sense of justice and mercy, both for relationships within the church and within the larger society. Even as we pray that we will be empowered to love one another and our neighbors with the unconditional love of Jesus Christ, we know that, being broken and imperfect people, we will fail. We understand that amidst diversity, being a community of wholeness requires that we be honest with each other and intentionally foster and participate in genuine dialogue; that we not avoid conflicts that arise among us but creatively and lovingly engage and confront such conflicts; that we remain willing to offer and receive forgiveness; and that each of us strive to be who God has created us to be and to see the beauty in each of our sisters and brothers. As we grow and live in Christ's love, we hope to be salt and light to those around us—bearing witness in word and deed to the love of God in Jesus Christ.

©Georgia Avenue Church

194

# Acknowledgements

I am acutely aware, as I have alluded to repeatedly in the letters contained in this book, that there are people in the broader church who have supported me on this journey. They have made it possible for me to be in this situation in which I could prosper in the ways I have written about, and I am most grateful to them. I cannot begin to name them all, but I could not have taken this journey if these dear people had not also been concerned to provide food and other aid for their brothers and sisters who were not so economically fortunate.

I also am indebted to many who read this manuscript and offered thoughtful suggestions, and encouraged me and held my hand, as it were, given all my insecurities about writing and publishing. I will name them in alphabetical order, praying that I am not forgetting any of you kind folks who have given me your time and energy to help with this project. So thank you so much, my dear wife, Barbara Antonoplos, and many friends for your generosity and counsel: Mary Anne Barton, Ed Bridges, Gordon Brooks, Stan Dawson, Helen Doerpinghaus, Gray Fitzgerald, Claire Hertzler, Sheldon Hurst, Wayne Kannady, Jonathan Larson, Emily Stewart, Jay Thomas, and my youngest children, Helen Hale and John Hale. I also want to recognize Walter Brueggemann, who some years ago read many of these letters and assured me they would be worth at least trying to publish. As you can imagine, encouragement from such a source is powerful, even though it has taken me so long to follow through. The contributions of all of these people were helpful and reassuring to keep me on the path.

I am grateful to Constance Hawkins' surviving siblings, Monica, Marlene and Harriet, who insisted that I use actual family names and made sure I had facts straight. They want the reader to know that all of them are drug free, Monica for 29 years, Harriet for 22 years and Marlene for 3 years.

Thank you, Mike Armstrong and Ella Duffy Haynes, for permission to include here the letters you wrote for a different purpose. Also, Robert Haynes, for such permission after Ella's passing.

All of us who have been involved in the food cooperative program owe a special debt of thanks to the Atlanta Community Food Bank, and most particularly Rob Johnson, COO for many years, for unswerving support of our organization and our families.

And finally, I must thank my mother for being the person who persisted in the church, the church that was used of God to bring me into relationship with Jesus. Thank you, Mother.

# Bibliography

Eller, Vernard, ed. *Thy Kingdom Come, A Blumhardt Reader*. Wm. B. Eerdmans Publishing Company, Grand Rapids, MI, 1980

May, Gerald, G. *The Awakened Heart*, HarperOne, New York, 1993

Peterson, Eugene. *Under the Unpredictable Plant: An Exploration in Vocational Holiness*. Wm. B. Eerdmans, Grand Rapids, MI 1992

Scripture quotations are from:

Made in the USA
Columbia, SC
08 March 2020

88896019R00126